ADVANCE PRAISE

"If Alex Ruziak's story of survival sounds miraculous, it is because
Jews in Nazi-occupied Slovakia needed a miracle—indeed multiple
miracles—to survive the horrors of genocide. Oren Schneider
mesmerizingly tells this story with compassion, suspense, and
meticulous attention to historical detail. But *The Apprentice of
Buchenwald* is more than the tale of a young man who prevailed
against all odds as his comfortable bourgeois life was upended by the
Nazis' Final Solution. It is also a thoughtful reflection on the
complexities of remembering, both for those who endured the trauma
firsthand, and those who grew up in its shadow. As Schneider learned
from his grandfather, optimism is the ultimate triumph. This is a
moving tribute to a grandfather who chose life in face of adversity,
one that many of us, grandchildren of those who miraculously
survived the Holocaust, never had the courage or tenacity to write.

– **Amir Goldberg, Associate Professor of
Organizational Behavior, Graduate School of Business,
Stanford University**

"The Apprentice of Buchenwald is an incredible story of courage and survival, meticulously researched and masterfully told. Oren Schneider's historically significant memoir of his grandfather is thrilling, riveting and totally unputdownable. Contemporary events make this book relevant today more than ever."

– Gilad Japhet, Founder, MyHeritage.com

"Being an inmate of a Nazi concentration camp did not stop Alexander Rosenberg. It did not stop him from doing whatever he could to keep his father alive. And it did not stop him from sabotaging the Nazi war effort by subtly tampering with the weaponry he assembled.

In telling this story, Oren Schneider does both of these things as well. He keeps his grandfather's memory alive. And he directly sabotages the efforts of those enemies of the Jewish people who deny the enormity of the Shoah, or who tell us that protection can be found in assimilation.

Read this work and hear the messages kept alive from a grandfather by his grandchildren and great-grandchildren, messages as relevant for the Jewish people today as they were when Alexander Rosenberg took up arms for the creation of the State of Israel:

Be grateful for life.

Believe in what you can accomplish.

And never rely on the world for your safety."

– Elisha Wiesel, son of Marion and Elie Wiesel

"Another stunning book released by Amsterdam Publishers is part memoir and part autobiography, written by the author, Oren Schneider, a detailed, beautifully written story about the author's grandfather's experiences before, during and after the Holocaust.

The first part of the book relates the story of Schneider's Jewish grandfather's elegant and successful life in Central Europe prior to World War II, the destruction of that life by local Hungarian Nazis and later German Nazis, the survival of Grandfather by his wits and talents and the reconstruction of his life in Israel after the war.

The second part of the book is the story of the author, a then self-absorbed young man, who connects with his grandfather in a deeply emotional way during a trip to Europe with his grandfather and the concentration camp in which his grandfather was incarcerated.

This is a deeply inspirational and moving book about how Grandfather's technical skills, language skills, personal courage and fearlessness led him to victory over his Nazi captors. The story is riveting, exciting and satisfying. The writing is superb as the author pulled me in to the story. I liked the occasional touches of humor that helped round out the personalities of both grandfather and grandson.

Many books are described as "page turners." This one really is. Once I started reading this book, I didn't put it down until I turned the last page. The book's subtitle is: "The true story of the teenage boy who sabotaged Hitler's war machine." It's true. Schneider's grandfather sabotaged hundreds if not thousands of Mauser rifles in collaboration with Russian POW's in the arms factory in which they all worked as slave laborers. There is a hint — unable to be confirmed — in the last section of the book, how the sabotage could have ironically boomeranged during Israel's War of Independence. *The Apprentice of Buchenwald* is suitable for upper-level high school students and adults. It is destined to become a classic. You really need to read it."

– Kenneth P. Price, Ph.D., psychologist and author of the award-winning *Separated Together. The Incredible True WWII Story of Soulmates Stranded an Ocean Apart.*

THE APPRENTICE OF BUCHENWALD

THE TRUE STORY OF THE TEENAGE BOY WHO
SABOTAGED HITLER'S WAR MACHINE

OREN SCHNEIDER

ISBN 9789493276604 (ebook)

ISBN 9789493276529 (paperback)

ISBN 9789493276536 (hardcover)

Publisher: Amsterdam Publishers, The Netherlands

info@amsterdampublishers.com

The Apprentice of Buchenwald is part of the series

Holocaust Survivor True Stories WWII

Copyright © Oren Schneider 2023

Cover image: Design by Allison Saltzman

Photographs cover © Valentino Sani / Trevillion Images (typewriter on chair) and Shutterstock (rifle)

CONTENTS

This book is a work of nonfiction. I have recounted the stories I heard growing up that my grandfather and great-grandmother told me about surviving during this horrifying period. Many of these stories are captured in detail in audio recordings. In a few cases, I've recreated scenes based on their recollections or, for narrative purposes, given names to people and places mentioned when their actual names are lost to history. If a person's thoughts are expressed, I drew my description of the person's thoughts from these stories I was told.

*To my beloved grandfather Alexander - I hereby fulfill your last wish;
your wounds and sacrifices are carved deep inside me; your life
philosophy made me the optimist I am*

*To Rio and Ruby, and a generation that can only read about the
Holocaust: never stop asking and challenging us, never forget the past
and never be indifferent to the suffering of those around you; make
your voices heard*

To my life partner Sharon, who taught me to feel

INTRODUCTION
BROOKLYN, 2023

I became an orphan at 15 months when my combat pilot father's plane, out on a scheduled training sortie, collided mid-air with a fighter jet. My mother, pregnant with my sister when the accident happened, never fully recovered.

My concentration camp survivor, maternal grandfather Alexander stepped into a father and educator role. He began sharing his World War II capturing and concentration camp survival stories with me when I was five. The year was 1980. Every Friday afternoon, lying next to each other on my grandparents' grand bed, he would uncover another layer, release another nerve, unveil another painful memory. Details of daily life in the Buchenwald concentration camp, mundane descriptions of a forced laborer's work shift in an armament factory, and stories about uncles and aunts who died in the gas chambers were as commonly discussed as latest soccer league standings or the soaring inflation in the Israeli economy. Growing up, I lived and breathed the annihilation, destruction and suffering endured by family and nation. Finding out that most children my age did not know, or were not closely related to a holocaust survivor, came as a surprise at first. Carrying the weight of memory became a calling. I started telling my family stories to my friends, and they always wanted to hear more.

Alexander's story is like no other. The project of documenting it began early, initially verbally, and later using recording devices. His mother Irena, already more than one hundred years old at the time but still sharp as a whip, was the only other character in the story to provide a recorded testimony. Alexander was doubtful of the world's desire to hear him out, but I never was. His story is worth telling because it is universal and timeless, depicting the loneliness and randomness of an individual's struggle against an evil of immense proportions. To me, it was always the feel-good tale of a person, left to their own devices against all odds and finding the inner strength to fight, rather than a tragic example of a persecuted Jewish family who managed to survive under the chaotic clouds of war.

COVID-19 brought tragedy, pain, and unprecedented economic loss to the people of the world. Our family had its own share. But COVID-19 also allowed me the space to travel back to 1980 and my grandfather's bed and restore the courage I had as a young boy to confront our heritage. In lieu of TV binging, I sat down to write, reliving every moment of his journey. I spent months researching, speaking with generations of family members who survived by making it to the United States before the war, and using these interactions alongside research conducted via MyHeritage.com to complete missing family pieces of the story. At the same time and half a world away, Alexander was taking his last breaths, quarantined, and separated from loved ones. He passed away just as my work had been completed. His last request from me, the last time we met in 2019, was to make sure his story is told.

Alexander (1927-2020) lived a full and rewarding life and was a hard-working and successful entrepreneur, oozing energy, optimism, and charm. But his soul was scarred and tainted beyond repair due to his childhood experiences. I could never separate Alexander the camp prisoner from head-of-the-family, Grandfather Alexander, who hustled and traveled the world to build a flourishing business and constantly push himself to prove his worth to himself. He remained a camp prisoner until his last day.

Photographs, recordings and additional materials about Alexander and his family can be found at www.ApprenticeOf-Buchenwald.com.

Never forget! Oren

PART 1
ALEXANDER

1 THE SMALL SQUARE I

1944, BUCHENWALD, THE THIRD REICH

The sun was setting slowly along the snowy hills and gloomy wooden structures surrounded by the thick barbed wires. The silence was broken intermittently by distant sounds of wild animals howling. The sky was clear, and the freezing wind was loud and persistent.

One by one, the 30-odd prisoners left their spots in the roll call once their names were announced and went inside the office in the wooden shed. Father was one of those prisoners. At least a dozen armed soldiers and a few German shepherd dogs were patrolling along the central administration building in the Main Camp. I was trying hard not to stare into their eyes.

And then there were only three of us left in the Small Square: a doe-eyed SS officer and two scrawny prisoners.

Only one prisoner was supposed to be standing there now, in front of the SS officer.

I was the odd man out, wearing a shabby concentration camp suit and lacerated, wooden-soled shoes.

There was nowhere to run this time. Even if there was, my two tired feet would not carry me far. The last few months forced Father and me into sticky situations only to escape by the skin of our teeth.

Alas, there was no way out this time for me, at least not one I could think of at that moment. I was very tired.

I vividly remember the thoughts running through my mind there and then. It occurred to me, for the first time since we were captured after years in hiding, that I didn't want to die at 17, namely because I was an only child, and Mother, if still alive, would not bear it. I saw her face in front of me. I didn't know where she was, if she was hungry or injured. It's been weeks since Father and I last saw her, when we were forcefully separated on the crowded railway platform in Nováky. Finally, it occurred to me that Father, who was taken through the office door just in front of me three hours ago, may already be dead.

The SS officer was staring silently at his notes for a few minutes.

The prisoner standing to my right was probably in his early twenties but looked much older. He resembled a tall, coat-hanger skeleton. His badge testified that he was a homosexual. I had never met homosexuals before arriving at camp. His skin was hanging from his collar bone, his shirt blowing in the wind as if it was completely hollow. He had a nervous facial twitch and was rocking his waist back and forth, fighting the cold or seeking stability. I must have looked as helpless and sickly as this abysmal creature did. His mad-looking, sad eyes were rolling from side to side, trying to make sense of the unfolding situation. Why is he not being called into the office after the rest of the pathetic group? What's going on?

The SS officer, blond and tall, full-bodied in his ironed uniform and probably only a few years older than me, flipped through his printed lists. By now, he was likely fully aware of the circumstances he was about to deal with. He then scratched the back of his head with a pencil and carefully examined the two prisoners standing in front of him. I knew that according to his notes, only the skin-and-bones prisoner to my right was supposed to be there. He gazed at my prisoner number again and again, then focused at the other prisoner's number.

Busted.

"You filthy Jew swine! You should be back in the Small Camp," he shouted at me and came closer. "What are you doing here? Who told you to join this group? I never called out your name or number this morning! What were you thinking?!"

Think, Alex, think. There was no light bulb turning on in my mind, so my default was groveling.

"I'm sorry, Mr. Officer, sir, please... I must have heard the wrong name being called out. Please forgive me, sir. My hearing is not well since my injury." I was blabbering, rambling, pleading for my life. No way this man is buying into my bullshitting.

Think, just think. I shut my eyes. Then it occurred to me how hungry I was.

I started daydreaming. In front of me, I saw heavenly Prague ham, sliced over a schmaltz-dripping fresh portion of pumpernickel bread, adequately sprinkled with fresh dill, on the counter in our family's delicatessen, and Irena Rosenberg, sitting there on the fine leather sofa, smiling, wearing her favorite Persian fur, cigarette at hand, puffing smoke and smiling at her son.

I didn't notice that the officer was now standing right next to me.

His first kick found my left rib cage and I fell to the ground, gasping in horror. In a furious burst of rage, he then started kicking my head, face, shoulders, back, and feet. I inhaled deeply and started screaming in a voice I couldn't recognize.

"Father! Help me! Help me! He is killing me!"

"Shout on! No one can hear your screams! You filthy, stupid, ugly Jew," he screamed as he continued kicking me. He sounded out of breath himself. "You are going to pay for this." His mouth was watery, and his teeth were clenched.

"Help me! Anyone!" I was screaming my lungs out.

Dear Mother, wherever you are, I'm so sorry, I won't be able to keep my promise. Feeble Father will be left to his own devices.

My eyes were shut. Now all I could see were the golden wheat fields surrounding my hometown of Sečovce, the shallow Trnavka river lazily flowing with a band of bees buzzing over the low shrubbery. I felt blood running all over my face as the rest of my body was frozen, bombarded with blows.

I will not make it back home. The bastards win.

Not more than seconds away now before losing consciousness, I was about to embark on my third train trip this month, this time to eternity.

2 A GOLDEN AGE

That afternoon in the snowy, Small Square, and the nightmarish months leading to it, came at a stark contrast to my early life experiences. My childhood was comfortable and pampering. Nothing in my upbringing had prepared me for the roll call outside of the city of Weimar that cold afternoon. I was a rather spoiled Czechoslovakian only child, raised in the lap of a vibrant, elevated German überculture. We were the sophisticated, enlightened folk. We were the economic and social elite.

I was born in 1927 in Sečovce, a small Eastern Slovakian town located close to both the Hungarian and Ukrainian borders. Both my parents came from Jewish trader families who owned and operated revered Main Street retail establishments in their respective hometowns. Like many brides during that time, my mother Irena moved to her husband's hometown of Sečovce from her nearby birthplace town of Trebišov after her wedding. She named me Alexander after her late father Alexander Rosenbaum, who never recovered following emergency stomach surgery in Vienna, just a few weeks before I was born. Everyone called me Sanyi (pronounced "Shun-Yi"), the common nickname of Sándor ("Shun-Door"), the

7

Hungarian form of Alexander. I probably had at least half a dozen cousins named Alexander.

My father Solomon Rosenberg was a grandson of the great rabbi of Tășnad, Rabbi Solomon Katz Rosenberg. The famous rabbi was born in 1840 and became leader of the Tășnad community in 1876. He died in 1898 and was buried in Tășnad. Known for his ultraconservative interpretations of the Talmud, my great-grandfather wouldn't approve of many of our family's secular life choices. My father made it clear to me early on that he didn't believe in the existence of God, but also said that I couldn't tell anyone about that, especially not family members. Keeping such a colossal secret felt like a big deal to me as a child.

Born and raised in Sečovce, Solomon, the youngest son in a family of eight, was the proud owner of his own namesake upscale "Solomon Rosenberg" delicatessen and specialty department store. His father, Bernat Rosenberg, the famous rabbi's son, owned and operated the upscale "Bernat Rosenberg" delicatessen and department store before him, and taught Solomon the secrets of the trade and the art of profiting from luxury goods. Father's three older brothers migrated to America well before I was born. His four sisters married and moved to their husbands' homes in Sečovce or in other district towns.

Solomon Rosenberg always wore a carefully pressed shirt, three-piece suit, and a tie. Always. When I was young, I believed he went to bed and woke up wearing a three-piece suit, because I rarely saw him without one.

Everyone called my father Zoli, except for Mother, whenever she was irked by him.

"Solomon!"

"Yes, dear?"

"You forgot to place the order for the special Belgian pralines that Katarina and Maria like! You know I'm hosting the card game tomorrow evening. I hate to constantly remind you of these things."

"Ah... so sorry. I was swamped at the store this week. It's the monthly inventory, as you know. I'll get a nice Sacher torte from Herschkowitz tomorrow afternoon. They'll lick their fingers, trust me."

Katarina was the Greek-Catholic bishop's wife and Maria was the wife of the Reform Church principal, and they were both my mother's close friends. She loved to host and had many close friends, most of them non-Jewish, high-society socialites, who seemed to enjoy Solomon Rosenberg's delicacies while smoking and playing cards in our expansive, modern living room. These fashionable women would sit in a cloud of smoke, long black velvet gloves holding on to their cigarette extenders and talk about the latest seasonal vogue trends to come out of Berlin, the fashion capital at the time.

My parents didn't have many Jewish friends, partly because we had a huge family that demanded much of our leisure time, but also because our household was very secular, unlike most of the homes belonging to our extended family members. One might call my parents closeted atheists. Most of the Jews in town, including most of our close family members, were true believers in the Hebrew God.

Other than the compulsory family events, including the High Holidays, my parents spent most of their spare time with like-minded Christian adults, who represented the region's aristocracy. The mayor, chief of police, and the Greek-Catholic bishop visited our home and store frequently.

"Sanyi, make sure you make friends at school. True friendships take years to cultivate and nurture. There is nothing more important than friends. Friendships elevate the soul," I remember her saying during a rare philosophical rant. She was usually a sharpshooter, practical and straight to the point, and didn't waste time on theoretical tirades.

"What makes a true friendship? Do you have true friends?" I wondered.

"True friendship means really knowing someone and connecting with them at a deep emotional level. It's about being there for them when they need you, not only when it's comfortable. I have a number of true friends, and that is because I dedicate my time and attention to them. I listen to them, and they listen to me. You should do the same."

"Does Father have true friends?"

"No. His only true friends are his business and his wife. I guess he doesn't really need other friends because he has us in his life. He has many people who respect him because of his integrity, success, and professionalism."

For Mother, style and sophistication were the secret recipe to living a satisfying, fulfilling, and respectable life. She always wore makeup, used the finest artisanal face and hand creams, brought to her on carriages by horsemen from farms around Slovakia, and a fresh eucalyptus scent followed her from room to room. Her clothes were tailored using the finest imported fabrics.

"Berlin, Sanyi, is the center of culture and style," she used to say. "Maybe we'll all go there for your Bar Mitzvah."

That would be something, indeed.

She collected beautiful, small things. I didn't care much for her assemblage of midget crystal characters or wooden figurines of farm animals. Those were all on display behind the grand living room vitrine. However, I was obsessed with the bronze statue of the two wide-eyed, long-eared French bulldogs, standing and gazing towards the horizon, which was placed next to the vitrine.

When I turned eight, Father allowed me to pick up the statue. I recall thinking that the artwork felt surprisingly cold, and that it was the heaviest, most condensed piece of anything I ever held in my hands. It was made by a local Gypsy artist and gifted by Father to Mother on their wedding day in 1926. A personal message and the year were engraved on the bottom. I followed the weld lines, scratches, and deformities with my fingers, and thought of the old artist in the rundown open-air village studio practicing his craft for a living.

Unlike his wife, Father cared little about collectibles. His passion lay in his trading business as well as in local politics revolving around our Jewish community.

"Why do we speak Hungarian at home? We live in Czechoslovakia!" I asked him one afternoon at the store.

"This is a smart question, Sanyi. Hungarian, like the German we also speak at home, is a language of high culture and education, unlike Slovak and Yiddish. Do you know what the word assimilation means?"

"I think I do," I answered doubtfully.

"Both your mother and I come from Jewish families who chose to assimilate. True, we go to shul on High Holidays, but we are not religious or observant. We own a business, and we are contributing members of a community of Christians and Jews who chose the path of education and liberalism."

"Why aren't all Jews like us?"

He smiled and paused. "Because our family is privileged, and fortunate enough to be wealthy. Slovakia is a poor land, unlike Moravia and Bohemia in Czechia that are very industrialized. Most Jews in Slovakia – and there are hundreds of thousands of them – are poor and uneducated. Most of them are very religious. We try to help them in any way we can. If you think about our small town – I would estimate our Jewish community at about 1,000 people, about a third of all residents. Many of them are well to do, but a considerable minority – and you see them lingering in shabby clothing around the center square – are very poor. But we are a well-organized community, and we help the ones in need. We pay for their Shabbat meals, and we make sure they have roofs above their heads."

Until that moment, I never thought of our family as privileged.

"Sanyi, you must finish all the food on your plate. Many children in town will not have any chicken, or any meat for that matter, for their Shabbat dinner."

That was a typical interpretation by my mother of our privileged status.

11

The Rosenbergs had lived in Sečovce for generations. Father owned a prayer book stamped with the name Urhersky Žipov, a small town on the Hungarian border. When I asked him about it, he said that our family came to Sečovce in the early 19th century from Urhersky Žipov. He kept that prayer book because it was his sole proof of the family's origin.

The Solomon Rosenberg specialty store was my magic kingdom, and I was its exclusive and distinguished knight. The business establishment was both my happy place and my worst enemy because it was my only sibling. My parents didn't want, or couldn't have, more children, so they raised one son and one store. We were constantly competing for adult attention. We played together and kept secrets from the world.

The store was located at the lower-level front of our family house in the town center. Both my parents worked there every day. I spent every free minute I had admiring the treasures and riches displayed on shelves and stored in credenzas. Imagine a private, shrunken version of Harrods in London, KaDeWe in Berlin, or Bergdorf Goodman in New York, all at my disposal, after hours. The store carried a wide selection of products: from the famous *Prager Schinken* [Prague ham], cut on a shiny and expensive electric slicing machine, and weighed on a fancy, modern yet ornamental Berkel scale and salted, fermented Scandinavian sour fish in small barrels, to expensive perfumes and leather luggage articles. The town's and region's finest frequented Solomon Rosenberg for self-pampering and indulgence.

While Father managed operations, Mother oversaw marketing and public relations. Every Christmas, I helped her create gift boxes that were sent to our best and most loyal customers. She curated legendary chocolate, toffee, and marzipan assortments, and added a personal touch with handwritten notes on elegant, Bavarian stationery.

My crown jewels were the exotic herbs and spices sold at the store, exquisitely ordered in small wooden drawers, which were marked and labeled. I could smell them from any corner of our house and from my bed upstairs at night. I used to dream of the faraway places where these spices came from.

"Cardamom... Cayenne pepper... Ceylon Cinnamon... Cilantro... Chili Pepper... Coriander seeds... Cumin..." I was proudly reciting spices that were stored in "C" section drawers from memory.

"You forgot 'capers'," said Father. "Nice job Sanyi, you will soon be able to start helping out with customers."

"Can I also please try operating the electric machine to slice the Prague ham?"

"Absolutely not. Using a dangerous blade involves precision work, and a child of five would do best to distance himself from sharp knives."

"You will be there to protect me."

"Absolutely not. Stay away from the knives. You should spend your free time reading and collecting your stamps."

He was not a risk-taker nor an adventurist. He was a trader, calculating risk against reward in every step.

From a young age, he encouraged and cultivated my stamp collection hobby. He used to set aside all kinds of envelopes and stamps from the store's business correspondence and bring them to me. He showed me how to dip the torn envelopes in water to neutralize the glue, separate and dry the stamps, and guided me on ordering them by date, geography, and themes.

My albums proudly included stamps from dozens of countries, none of them I had ever visited, but from where the delicacies were shipped to our store. I mapped German, British, French, Italian, Spanish, Indian and Moroccan stamps to culinary delights, large and small, on the shelves.

Our house at 152 Štefánikova Street was more than 200 years old. It had three large storefronts with lofty glass windows, and a small gate in the corner of the lot, leading to the backyard. From the yard, there was access to our home and to a few rental properties that were leased out.

Our family unit was large and spacious, with a well-organized, modern kitchen, five bedrooms, a lavatory, and a bathroom built by my father, equipped with one of the town's first, state-of-the-art electrical water pumps. This was a completely new concept, as the town did not have central water supply. Our guests curiously admired the astounding invention, which I passionately volunteered to demonstrate.

The backyard had a water well and a manual water pump, as well. For cooking, our maid still pumped water into buckets and brought them into the kitchen.

I remember my father marching ahead of a construction crew, to build a concrete sewage pit, where the sewage water would run, in the backyard. The water was absorbed back into the ground through the layer of soil at the bottom of the pit. The remaining waste was emptied by a wagon driver using a huge bucket, every other year. That waste was used, for the most part, to fertilize our vegetable shrubs.

My parents employed a household staff of two women. One was responsible for cleaning the house and cooking, and the other took care of me. I had had a nanny since birth, and we spent hours together every day, because Mother was at the store. My nannies were often replaced because Mother had high standards. I especially recall one of them because she, a devout Catholic, only spoke German. My grandmother Jolan, Father's mother, also only spoke German. They were both wide women, who always dressed in black and spent much time together. That nanny would drag me with her on every Catholic funeral march going through main street, walking after the casket in a carriage, until Father, white as limestone, happened to walk on the street while the parade was marching on, and saw me there. That was the last funeral I attended. Our cook was masterful. Her specialty was the Slovak classic peasant delicacy, *bryndzové halušky* [sheep milk cheese dumplings], which she would make from scratch every week. When we were hosting larger parties, she would prepare rich goulash soups, stuffed pierogi, and pork schnitzels or pork with dumplings and cabbage. As secular Jews, we regularly ate pork at home, but never spoke of it outside.

"Your father is a good man and a hard worker. But he can be stubborn as an ox and inflexible at times. Don't be as naive as he is."

"What do you mean, Mother?" I didn't understand what would make her say something like that about Father.

"Nothing. Just promise me to keep an eye on him." Keeping an eye on my father? On more than one occasion she repeated this or similar sentiments, and I couldn't understand why.

Town life was peaceful and tranquil in the early 1930s. On summer weekends, the town center was filled with families, walking around, and chatting with neighbors and friends.

The men's regional pastime was soccer. Father loved watching our local team play, and I loved witnessing him cheer enthusiastically from the stands. That was the only place where he allowed himself to loosen up, no longer being the three-piece-suit-Solomon-Rosenberg. He would shout and curse at the other team, and I used to laugh so hard. The municipal stadium had a plain wooden bar separating the grass pitch from the spectator seats. He often used to take me on weekends to attend games, especially when their archrivals, the team from Trebišov, would visit. They used to call the Trebišov squad "The Knives," because every time an argument or quarrel started on the pitch, knives would come out.

The main Jewish synagogue was the fanciest, most decadent building in town. Being a family of Kohanim [members of the priestly class of Judaism], we had dedicated front-row seats in the Eastern Wing, adjacent to the Torah, on every High Holiday. Father was adamant about maintaining the traditions of Jewish holidays. On Yom Kippur, he would wear his white kittel, and my grandmother would assume her honorary seat on the top floor in the *Ezrat Nashim* [women's section]. I used to bring her a flower to the synagogue, and she always pretended to be surprised by it.

The town had a Jewish school, Catholic school, Reform school, and a government-run public school. The Jewish elementary school I attended was adjacent to the synagogue. All teachers were Orthodox Jews, and the curriculum was approved and supervised by the liberal government of Czechoslovakia. Studies were rigorous, and the children were highly disciplined. I was slapped with a ruler more than once for passing notes during class.

Morning classes focused on general studies, math, languages, science, and history. Slovak was the formal spoken language at school. In the afternoons, we went to the heder to learn the Bible with the rabbi. I hated these long afternoons, as the languages spoken in our house were primarily Hungarian and German, and Bible lessons were strictly in Yiddish. The rabbi, like many other Jewish members of the community, mainly communicated in Yiddish. He would translate biblical verses from Hebrew to Yiddish and get upset with me for having to add a Hungarian translation, for my Yiddish wasn't as fluent.

"*Razenberg, du hist a goy!*" [Rosenberg, you are a gentile!]

"*Neyn, ikh bin nisht, har.*" [No, I'm not, sir.]

"*Azoy vos deyn eltern zen bloyz goyim?*" [So why are your parents only being seen with gentiles?]

"*Ikh vise nisht, har.*" [I don't know, sir.]

We got together with family members every week. Especially with Grandmother Rosenberg, when she was still alive.

During family gatherings and holiday meals, there was constant arguing and convincing about the future and destiny of our Czechoslovakian Jewish community. There were always three distinct camps around the table, as termed and explained to me by my parents. First, there were the Traditionalists, who saw Czechoslovakian Jews as an indispensable fabric of local society, a pillar of the community, leading the economy in areas such as medicine, law, and trade. Second, the New World Prophets, who were captivated by the freedoms promoted and advertised by the United States. Every family with some degree of means had at least one son (but never a daughter) who had left town on a voyage that ended on a boat to America. Third and last were the Zionists, who saw the future of Judaism in Palestine. In the 1920s, Europe began witnessing a birth of various Zionist youth movements, of which the best known were *Beitar* and *Hashomer Hatzair*. These movements advocated the immigration of Jews to Palestine so that a national home for Jews could be re-formed in their old, biblical Promised Land. The Zionist movements were closely aligned with socialist ideas, and some of their leaders sought to take their cues directly from the Comintern in Moscow.

Three of my father's brothers left for America a decade before I was born, before and during World War I. Many of his nephews did the same. We did not, however, have close family members who were Zionists.

Uncle Itsu, Mother's older brother, always said that the country would collapse without the dynamic participation of "hardworking, entrepreneurial Jews" from the labor force, who had been "the backbone of the Slovak economy." He despised and ridiculed the two other groups.

"Father, did you ever think about immigrating to America?"

"Not really, no. All I ever wanted was to start my own business, and we had all the resources and contacts to be successful here at home."

"Did you and Mother ever consider joining any of the Zionist movements? Or immigrating to Palestine?"

"Heavens, no. These socialists are dangerous. The central government will someday crack down hard on them. As for Palestine, this is not a place you really want to go to. The Levantine or Arab culture, the hot and humid weather, the religious wars, why would we want a piece of that? We have everything we will ever need here in Czechoslovakia."

Life was good in Sečovce.

I spent my long summer vacations with Grandmother Theresa in Trebišov, which was only a 15-minute train ride from our town.

Mother's Trebišov-based immediate family, the Rosenbaums, was composed of more than 100 people, and had a reputation for being strikingly tall and handsome. Grandfather Rosenbaum himself had 11 brothers and sisters. The family lived in Trebišov for many generations, was exceedingly wealthy, and owned several palatial mansions. I was introduced to dozens of family members there every summer. The Rosenbaums were much fancier than the Rosenbergs.

My grandmother's brother owned a large agricultural farm near Sečovce, on the main road leading to Košice. Another uncle owned an entire tobacco-growing village named Hradište, gifted to his family by a local nobleman, as gratitude for "services provided to the motherland." That branch of the family had been the largest supplier of cigarettes to the government of Czechoslovakia.

I used to spend time in Hradište during my childhood, walking around the modern machinery and huge wooden silos, which were used to dry up the tobacco. Tobacco plants grow higher than those of corn, and Father repeatedly warned me about them. He said that if a child entered a huge tobacco field and lost their way, they may never be found alive, and warned me to not venture into the fields. To bring this warning to life, my uncle walked me five yards into the plantation, and I completely lost all orientation.

Mother was born in 1907, when Trebišov was still part of the Austro-Hungarian Empire. The region became part of Czechoslovakia after the conclusion of World War I. She grew up homeschooled with a private Hungarian tutor and a young German teacher, who taught language and culture. Her grandparents from both sides only spoke German, the civilized language of high society. Their vast book library was in German. She studied piano in German and went to see plays, theater, and chamber concerts, exclusively in German.

My grandfather Alexander Rosenbaum owned the town's main department store, where my mother and her 11 siblings worked. My extremely well-to-do grandparents lived across the street from Mother's family.

During the Great War, when the Russians were nearing Trebišov, Mother's family fled to Budapest for a few months, before returning home. Grandfather Alexander spent three years fighting for the Austro-Hungarian army during the war, which is when he contracted the stomach disease that led to his eventual, untimely demise. Mother would always tell me about that cursed day in 1916, when her mother read aloud from the paper that Emperor Franz Josef had passed away, and how she cried out of anxiety for things to come, and the uncertain future awaiting her offspring. Mother often spoke of the Great War and the hard times they experienced when her father was away fighting. Short on food and supplies, the family's diet was corn-based. They used corn to bake bread and cakes and to fix themselves porridge. Once a week, on Thursdays or Fridays, they would bake challah for Shabbat. The family was not very religious, but Shabbat was always respected. Her mother would make sure they had meat and cake on Shabbat. After the war, her father came back from the front, reopened the family store, and things gradually went back to normal.

"Thankfully, Sanyi, you will not need to experience the devastation of a world war such as the Great War. The famine. The death. The loss of loved ones. The cruelty. The carnage. We now live in a new world," she would say.

Mother married at 19, two weeks before her father passed away. After she moved in with Father in Sečovce, her older brother Itsu, who was a bank clerk, left his job to take over the family business after Grandfather's funeral.

I loved music. Neither of my parents were very musical, although Mother played the piano her entire childhood. She forced me to take violin lessons from a young age. The moment I saw that delicate instrument, it was love at first sight. My teacher, a well-known, local Gypsy musician who played in regional concerts and familial gatherings, visited us twice a week for my lessons. He was a master of his trade, with a voice as pure as a nightingale's. He taught me to play with my heart and introduced me to Gypsy folk music. He also encouraged me to sing at every opportunity. He told me I had a beautiful voice.

"Alexander! Please come down and play a song for the dear ladies," Mother called from the living room. This was not spontaneous by any means, and we had rehearsed the scene that very morning.

"Coming!" Prepared and ready for her invitation, I trotted down the stairs wearing my best jacket, proudly holding on to my violin.

"Good evening, Ma'am, Ma'am," I bowed in front of Katarina and Maria. "I will sing and play *Under our window*."

Soon a sweet tune filled the room.

Under our window,
tends to be very cold.
Our well is frozen,
and water isn't flowing.

I'll take my little hatchet,
and break the ice layer.
And in our well,
water will flow again.

Under our window,
Is a white rose flower.
Tell me, my dear,
What troubles you so.

I'll take my little hatchet,
and break the ice layer.
And in our well,
water will flow again.

Under our window,
a white Lilia.
Tell me, my dear,
who comes for you.

I'll take my little hatchet,
and break the ice layer.
And in our well,
water will flow again.

I bowed.

"Bravo, Alexander, well done," said Maria.

"Time to go to bed. Your father and I are pleased with your progress with the violin," said Mother and turned her head to face her friends.

That was as big a compliment as I ever got from her.

Those were the best of times. Czechoslovakia's golden age.

We didn't feel different as Jews.

My parents constantly referred to our country as Europe's improved, civilized version of the United States. Mother mocked Father's brothers for jumping ship and schlepping to America in the belly of an immigrant boat through Ellis Island, to turn over a new leaf as penniless nomads who didn't speak the local language.

"What were they missing here? We live at the epicenter of culture, music, food, and style. I don't want to go to Yonkers."

I had no idea where Yonkers was and later found out this was a city in New York State where one of our cousins had immigrated to.

She didn't see the great ball of fire heading our way. None of us did. It came as fast as the streaming rain.

3 THE FALL

My parents never discussed politics at home. Dinner talks often focused on complimenting Mother on her masterful recipes and menu selection, the business, our customers, family news from throughout the region, community events and activities, and my day at school. Our world was confined to the boundaries of the regional capital of Košice.

If my parents had any anxieties about the worrisome developments in Nazi Germany during the 1930s, they kept them all to themselves.

Until that one late afternoon when I was nine, and Father walked into the house.

"Zoli, is something wrong? You look very pale. Here, please have some water."

He walked into the living room and looked like he had been struck by lightning.

"I'm fine," he answered after taking a long breath. "Just got back on the train from Košice. Someone posted a sign at the train station entrance that called for all Jews to leave Czechoslovakia. A properly printed sign! Can you believe that? I just stood there and couldn't believe my eyes. That was incredibly disturbing to read. I'm still shocked."

Loud silence.

"Sanyi is here, let's talk about this later, please," she replied.

It wasn't often that my presence would alter a topic of discussion at home. I was much intrigued now. "Who put up that sign? Who would want Jews to leave Czechoslovakia? Why?"

"It's rather complicated," he stuttered, looking for the right words. "There are people, well, who are angry because they are poor and are, the way they see it, mistreated by our government... They don't like Jews because they think Jews are rich and powerful, and made their wealth inappropriately."

"But we are rich, aren't we?"

He smiled and was increasingly uncomfortable. "Yes, that is true, Son. Our family lives a comfortable life because your mother and I, like our parents and our grandparents before us, work very hard, every day, to earn a living. Nothing dishonest about that."

"But there are also rich people who are not Jewish in town."

"As I said, this is really complicated. Many times, throughout our people's history, we have been persecuted because of our religion. But just like during those dark times, these troubles too shall pass."

"And who is Adolf Hitler?"

Loud silence, once again.

"Where did you hear that name? We never mentioned him by name at home."

She was giving me her furrowing look.

"Erno told me last week at school that Adolf Hitler was a very bad and rude German man, who claims that all of Europe's problems were caused by Jews."

"Well, Erno should know better than to discuss these things at school," said Mother, taking back control of the conversation assertively. "Adolf Hitler is an uneducated Austrian riffraff, and the proper authorities in Germany know exactly how to handle these good-for-nothing saboteurs. We will not mention that name in this house ever again. End of discussion."

Actually, it turns out that we did end up mentioning that name from that day on. Plenty of times.

The national and regional publications were reporting the horrific news coming out of Berlin and all of Germany, spreading into Nazi-friendly regimes around Europe. I never saw Father as baffled as he was when reading aloud an article about the Anschluss. Later that same year, his voice cracked during dinner while reading reports following *Kristallnacht* [the so-called Night of Broken Glass], when dozens of Jews were murdered, hundreds of synagogues burned, and thousands of Jewish-owned businesses were attacked, burned, looted, and destroyed throughout Germany.

Violence crept closer to home.

We started witnessing the presence of a new, radical Slovakian nationalist, antisemitic group named *Hlinkova Garda* [the Hlinka Guard]. The group was named after a Catholic priest named Hlinka. They persecuted all "foreigners" in our region, but mainly focused on Jews and Gypsies. The *Garda* took its cues from the German Nazi party, mimicking their methods of humiliating and taunting Jews. Father explained to me that Hlinka's leaders, among them Ferdinand Ďurčanský and Alexander Mach, were seeking Slovakian autonomy and were siding with the German-Czech residents of the Sudetenland in their demand to be annexed to Germany.

One afternoon I was working on my homework in our store when a stranger, wearing the *Garda* uniform, came in. Mother was standing at the counter. Father was out of town for a business meeting.

"Where can I find the Jew Solomon Rosenberg?"

I saw her looking at me and then turning her head back towards the stranger.

"The owner is not here at the moment, sir," she replied laconically.

"The owner? What a joke," he said. He spat on the counter and continued. "We'll just need to see about that. Won't you send him a message from the *Hlinkova Garda*? Tell him to close shop by tomorrow, take his family, and go elsewhere. I will be back to make sure he does that."

He looked at both Mother and me, and it was clear he figured out the family connection. The vulgar stranger then left, and her face turned strawberry red. She didn't speak another word until Father came back home.

Who was that man? I had never heard anyone speak to my parents, or to any adult for that matter, in such an aggressive and violent manner.

That evening, Father left home to meet with Franz, the mayor of Sečovce, and a close friend of my parents, to report the incident. Franz had also been our store's best customer. He never paid for any product he bought, though. He came back late in the evening and joined us around the dinner table.

"What did Franz say, Zoli?"

"He said that we should relax and forget about the whole thing. Apparently, it was an honest mistake. Just a simple misunderstanding. The local *Hlinkova Garda* office didn't have our details and credentials, and they should not have paid us a visit today."

"Are you saying that they are making similar visits to all Jewish businesses in town? Has the world gone completely mad?"

"I know. These are dark times. We must lay low until this storm calms down. There is really not a lot we can do."

"But how can you be sure they won't be back? This man was dangerous. I was so scared! You should have seen him, listened to his tone of voice. They are violent brutes."

"I can't be sure, but we have to put our trust in Franz. He says he will protect us. That's exactly why we've been treating him well for so many years."

Listening to this loaded discussion, this last sentence struck a deep chord.

"What did you mean by that? You have allowed the mayor to buy products without paying because you knew we would need his protection? How could you have known that the *Garda* would threaten us?", I asked.

They were caught completely off guard.

"You misunderstood Father's words, Sanyi. He didn't mean it the way you understood it. All he was saying is that Franz is our friend and will take care of us."

"No, but he said that–"

"Enough, I misspoke," said Father, cutting me off.

"I'm so scared, Zoli."

I never thought Mother would be scared of anything or anyone. Usually, everyone was scared of her. She was the toughest person I knew.

That *Garda* thug never came back to visit us after that day, but the following days and weeks we started hearing how the *Garda* and the *Freiwillige Schutzstaffel* (FS), the Voluntary Protection Corps, a local Slovak paramilitary group, were becoming increasingly violent and hostile towards Jewish business owners in Sečovce. There were organized campaigns to boycott Jewish stores and gut-wrenching stories of property confiscation. Mother said on a number of occasions that many ordinary folks had simply joined the *Garda* and FS to participate in the "organized, government-sponsored looting" of Jewish property, mainly real estate and operating businesses.

Events around us were unfolding at a frantically fast pace.

The Munich Agreement ended any illusion my parents had that Czechoslovakia could escape the annexation fate of its eastern neighbor, Austria. The British, French, and Italians allowed Germany to scoop and annex the Sudetes Mountain area with its population. Unopposed, the German Army entered Czechoslovakia and announced the creation of the Protectorate of Bohemia and Moravia. That prompted the *Garda* announcement of an independent Slovak state, and for the first time in my life, I started hearing my parents mutter, what was up until a few months ago, the unthinkable.

"Irena, we must think about leaving the country. I didn't think it would come to this, but we must reconsider our life here."

"I understand that, but where could we go, Zoli? Our whole life, family and business are here."

"I don't know. Maybe Switzerland? The United States? Australia? I get a sense that the situation here could get much, much worse for us. even dangerous. I'm worried for our safety."

"Do you think we could sell the business? What do you think we could get for it?"

"I don't know."

"Who would buy it?"

"I don't know."

"How can we find out?"

"Honestly, I don't know. I fear that if Franz learns that we were looking to leave town, we may discontinue any preferential treatment towards us, and the business would be lost altogether."

I couldn't believe they were having that discussion in front of me. Their words didn't scare me or trigger any anxieties. It felt like being a spectator in a movie, following the hero and heroine making life-altering decisions under threat of persecution. It didn't feel as if my life was at stake. I was almost 12 then.

They then had several follow-up discussions about the uncertainty of life, the shrinking options we were facing, and a future in utter limbo. They couldn't figure out how to liquidate our property, which was critical because they wouldn't leave without money. Father suggested once that we give up the store and goods and just leave, but Mother wouldn't hear of leaving with only her jewelry and a few gold pieces.

"When did you last speak to Franz? Are we safe?" She asked that question every other day. He would always reply that we were, indeed, safe, for the time being.

'With the creation of the autonomous Slovak state, wheels were in motion to legalize the transfer of all Jewish property to Aryan hands. One day, Father came home and sat us down in the kitchen to update us following his weekly meeting over tea with Franz in the municipal building.

"I bring more bad news, unfortunately," he said. "I was forced to agree to immediately bring in an *Aryzator* to the business."

"What *is that?*" asked Mother.

"An *Aryzator* is an Aryan, non-Jewish, business owner," he answered. "Franz told me that the new government is about to pass a law that forbids Jews from owning any type of business. Unless we voluntarily suggest a non-Jewish person as the majority owner of our business, the local authorities will arbitrarily assign us one by the first day of next month."

She held her head and started sobbing quietly.

"Dear, everything will be okay. Franz promised he would find someone friendly who would allow us to continue working and earning a living from the business. That person would walk away, no questions asked, when all this craziness subsides." He put his hand on her shoulder.

I'd never seen my parents touch each other in front of me before. We weren't a touchy-feely, warm, and physical type of family. I can't recall the last time she hugged me. I must have been very young.

"Do you even listen to yourself?" she whispered back. "Someone we don't know, who is likely a member of the *Garda*, would 'allow us to continue working and earning in our business'? This is insane."

"I know, I know." His hand was on her shoulder, and he seemed ready to collapse himself. He didn't.

The next day, the police chief visited the store accompanied by a short, plump woman I'd never seen before. She introduced herself in a pleasant voice as Margaret, and seemed nice, and her demeanor and appearance reminded me of our onion trader in the food market. I instantly assumed we were just introduced to the new owner of our family business. Our very own, private *Aryzator*. That evening I learned more about Margaret. She was the wife of one of the town's taxi drivers, a senior *Garda* activist. Our life and destiny were now at the hands of a stranger, most likely an avid antisemite.

As of the following morning, Margaret started showing up to work, never missing an hour of operation. Father forfeited and yielded to her all copies of the keys to the store, both from inside our house and from the street entrance. She would sit at the cash register, and put all money collected from sales into her coat pocket. The business deteriorated rather quickly, and Father no longer had any say in the daily operations of his store, including management of, and payments to, suppliers, product assortment, or product display. More critically, he lost his long-standing ability to gift luxury products to local politicians and officials, to protect us.

"Stop! Alexander Rosenberg, keep away from the herb drawers. I don't want you touching anything in my store without my permission."

That was that. I bid farewell to my kingdom, my only sibling. You've been kind to me. Your knight is submitting his resignation letter. Sorry for abandoning you to the graces of this chubby woman.

In spite of the humiliating situation with Margaret, we knew we were the lucky ones compared to other Jewish families who owned businesses. Because of Franz's introduction and promise to my father, our *Aryzator* was familiar with our family and probably had some level of respect towards us. She let us enjoy a modest weekly allowance that afforded us food and clothes. Still, our business no longer generated a proper livelihood for us. We had let go of the help at home. We started having meat only once a week, for Shabbat dinner. The rest of the time it was cabbage and potatoes.

At some point, the *Garda* also renamed the streets in the town center. Ours was no longer called Štefánikova; from now on the street sign read HLINKOVA, which was more in keeping with the zeitgeist.

The months went by.

After graduating from Jewish elementary school, I enrolled in the public junior high school, which taught its curriculum in German, a

29

language each Czechoslovakian child had to master. I spent 18 months there, until all Jewish children were legally prohibited from attending state-operated schools. At that time, the Jewish school was already shut down at the order of the *Garda*, and Jewish kids had practically nowhere to study. Now that I also became a persona non grata at *Solomon Rosenberg*, I spent my days walking around town. Father, worried about my education and personal development, arranged for me to start an apprenticeship with a neighbor, who was a Jewish locksmith.

He sat me down at our yard for a pep talk. "I know you will work hard and learn a useful trade. I also know you will not disappoint us."

"I won't, I promise."

"You are becoming a man, and as you start your professional career, we wanted to give you something." He handed me a small, elongated box. It was a Doxa watch. I was caught off guard because it had been a long while since gifts or any types of gestures had been exchanged, or events celebrated, in our home.

"Thank you, I promise I won't disappoint you."

He gave me a long hug, for the first time in a long while.

I loved my days with the old locksmith. He was a white-haired artist with magical hands who taught me how to use homemade tools to manipulate wood and metal, how to weld, dismantle simple and complicated locks, apply oil into analog mechanisms to maintain their movement, and how to create a tidy and orderly environment for my tools. Like Father, he reiterated the importance of order and discipline. Every afternoon I would come back home from his studio with a black face, dirty hands, and a wide smile.

"Young man, you have the most capable pair of hands of all apprentices I have had the pleasure to mentor in the last 40 years. You are also a hard worker and well-mannered. I'm sure your parents are proud of you. You will get far in life, maybe even have your own locksmithing business at some point," the old man told me one day as we were cleaning up and getting ready to close.

That was the nicest thing any person had ever said to me. By far.

I had no idea my hands were capable, or that, compared to my peers, people would consider me a hard worker. My parents didn't really believe in positive reinforcements or compliments of any kind. Most likely, their parents hadn't either. Mother had, however, plenty of criticism directed at me. I'd always been micromanaged at home.

"You've been cooped up in your room for hours with your stamps, please go outside to get some fresh air."

"You've been walking outside for hours and told no one where you were going. You should spend most of your time at home. How about working on that stamp collection, or practicing the violin?"

"Don't eat all the cabbage and potatoes, we need to start rationing our consumption."

"You haven't eaten anything, you're looking pale. You must eat more. Take some more potatoes. How about some cabbage?"

"How did you manage to stain the Shabbat shirt again? You should be more responsible, we're not here to serve you."

The locksmith was the first person who treated me as an adult.

Just when we thought that life had stabilized into a predictable and manageable routine, and that things couldn't turn out to be any worse, Hitler invaded Poland. The Second World War had begun.

While a world war was a novelty for me, my parents carried plenty of stories and scars from the Great War. They spoke of famine, loneliness, and unspeakable wartime cruelty that inflicted endless suffering and pain among civilians. They also said that it was unthinkable that humanity would find itself in the same pit of despair it had just barely climbed out of, less than 20 years before.

The new Slovak government in Bratislava established the Slovakian Gestapo (USB) that applied the German playbook for anti-Jewish activities. They forbade Jews from owning land and real estate. We were prohibited from going to the theater, entering the parks, or accessing food markets during certain hours of the day. All

Jewish organizations were outlawed and shut down. Jewish property, including real estate, jewelry, and personal belongings, was confiscated. Government regulations enforced the obligatory wearing of the Jewish yellow star, matching the legal definition of a Jew to that of the Nuremberg Race Laws. We had to travel in dedicated train cars and obtain a written license if we wanted to leave town.

Because non-Jewish Slovak men were enlisted in the Slovak army and joined the *Wehrmacht* [the German Army], there was a need for laborers for building roads, bridges, and tunnels. Jewish men from all around the country were identified and obligated to fill that void. All Jewish men between the ages of 20 and 50 were required to report to labor camps. Mother and I celebrated my Bar Mitzvah at home around the table, as Father spent 45 days away from home, working on one of these projects. We never got to go on that Bar Mitzvah trip to Berlin.

When he came back, dark-tanned, and exhausted, my parents went to the municipality building to hand over all our gold. They had to sign a formal affidavit confirming that they had retained none of the precious metal. Penalty for a false statement was death.

Then the *Garda* representative came by to let us know they were going to confiscate our beautiful furniture. For Mother, this was equivalent to seeing her soul crushed and smashed into a million tiny pieces.

"Irena, according to the leaflets they handed out today, we need to hand over all the furniture immediately." Father, aware of the sensitivity, spoke quietly.

Silence.

"No! I will not give them the furniture."

Two days went by.

"Irena, the *Garda* will either come and take everything any day now, or I can ask Franz to let them know we are handing over the furniture to Katarina and Maria."

"I know. I already spoke to both yesterday," she answered, dreary eyed. "I explained that we will give them the furniture for safekeeping, until we are allowed to take it back. They said they are happy to help. They are coming with the horseman tomorrow."

The brown leather sofa was the last to go into the wagon. Maria hugged my weeping mother and promised her that once this "insanity" passed, our furniture would be returned, along with our "life normalcy," to us. Watching Maria from the top of the staircase, I didn't believe she meant what she had said.

Our home was left almost barren.

"Mother, how come your friends couldn't help us keep our furniture?"

"They couldn't, Sanyi, they just couldn't," she answered with little conviction. "These are orders coming down from the government in Bratislava."

"Couldn't they leave us a few of our chairs, or maybe the dining table? Did they have to take everything but our beds?"

"I don't know, Sanyi. I don't want to speak about this anymore."

A few weeks later, Margaret our *Aryzator* took sole possession of the store with her husband. A *Garda* person accompanied them inside one morning and told my father we were no longer allowed back in the store, and that our stipend would be discontinued effective immediately. Again, he sought Franz's help, but there was nothing he could do for us.

We started hearing of mass deportations of Jews from all over Slovakia. But where were they being deported to?

Spending hours together in a lightless, empty apartment, my parents shared dark news received from family members and acquaintances in surrounding towns and villages. Thousands of Jews were concentrated at the order of the police and the USB, put on trains, and deported northbound to Poland. No one knew where they were going, and no news came from the travelers. Father asked me to leave my apprenticeship and always stay indoors. He was the only one in the family who left home to buy groceries.

Even though most of our property and income were taken away from us, our family was nevertheless one of the very few who were granted a White Certificate, or certificate of exemption, given to Jews who are "essential" for maintaining the daily operations of the Slovak nation, and were therefore not to be deported.

I was awakened early on a sunny day by a loud knocking on the front door. It was a damned day none of us will ever forget.

It was May 5, 1942.

Father opened the door, and Franz the mayor walked in hastily.

"Zoli, apologies for the early-hour interruption. For a long time, I feared this day would come. I wanted to personally let you know that late last night a German Army battalion arrived and is now camped at the main entrance to town. We just received orders to gather all Jewish families and march them through main street to the train station entrance this morning."

He paused and then added, "Train cars are ready and waiting at the station for the families, and they will be heading north this evening, to Poland."

He then said that the local SS field commander had granted the town leadership the prerogative to name ten Jewish families that were essential to the economy and would be spared deportation and allowed to remain in town, unharmed. The mayor himself compiled the list and our family was included as one of the ten. He repeatedly asked my father not to worry.

Mom was standing next to me at the edge of the stairway on the second floor, and we were listening to the conversation.

"Whatever you do, Zoli, do not leave the house today. Tell Irena and your boy not to go out. If anyone comes knocking, especially the Germans, show them the White Certificate and ask them to speak with me. I will be at the train station all morning."

Father hadn't muttered a single word.

"I will be attaching this official notice to your front door, to inform the SS that the residents of this house are not candidates for deportation and that you should not be taken to the train station."

Franz left as swiftly as he came in.

It felt as if all the oxygen had been sucked out of our home instantaneously. Father was left frozen, holding on to the front doorknob. Mom was sitting on the floor next to me, staring at the brick wall.

"Can they force us to go on the trains to Poland?"

"No Sanyi, we are safe, for the time being." He climbed up the stairs and stood next to me. "Whatever you do son, don't go outside today. Don't even look outside. Today is a terrible, cursed day."

My parents went into their bedroom and shut the door behind them.

It didn't even occur to me to look outside when listening in to Father's and Franz's discussion. But now that Father had made it a point to plead that I don't peek, I naturally couldn't help myself. Where would I have the best view of the street?

Our house was situated right on main street, but our unit did not have any windows facing the street itself. I decided to climb up to the roof.

The scenes from that morning will forever be carved in my memory, as much as I tried to eradicate them. A line of people was progressing slowly towards the train station. Among them were friends from my school, my teachers, our baker and his family, our family doctor and his family, families with babies, young children, women, and men, young and old, walking along in a straight, orderly line through the street, down to the station, carrying suitcases and bags. They just kept on coming. German soldiers made sure no one broke rank. They were all walking peacefully and quietly, at a slow and constant pace. My heart was pounding. It was completely surreal.

The stream of people began thinning. I started hearing noises and shouting from our backyard, so I climbed down to see what the commotion was about.

Our apartment had a small window facing the neighbor's yard. The man was in the shoe and leather business. He was an old, albeit strong, man, who we used to call Uncle Alexander. He was a widower. I stared out through the window. Uncle Alexander was standing with his back to the wall, shouting at three German soldiers who were standing next to him.

"I fought for Kaiser Wilhelm, side by side with the German Army... I was a loyal soldier... I have citations! I have medals! I can show you! You can't force me to leave my home!"

It did not help. A man in SS uniform hit him twice in the face and he fell down, sobbing. They kicked and hit him again, dragging him out of the yard to the street. They forcefully led his two daughters after him.

I went to bed and fell asleep. When I woke up it was already late afternoon. I climbed back on the roof. The street was desolate. Not a cat was walking around. I couldn't tell whether the morning commotion had been real, or if I was dreaming all this time.

The town became empty of its Jewish inhabitants, and about a third of its population, overnight, and our sadness and horror knew no boundaries. We did not leave the house for days, eating rationed preservatives. We couldn't bring ourselves to step out to the streets of our own town. We mourned the loss of our community, without knowing where those families were destined to go. We assumed that all our family members from Trebišov, Michalovce, Hradište, Košice, and other nearby towns had been captured and included in the transports. None of them had a White Certificate. We mourned our inescapable fate. We knew we were living on borrowed time and that they would be coming for us eventually. The rumor mill claimed that the trains that carried the town Jews were en route to the Lublin area in Poland, but we couldn't make any sense of it.

The town's main street, which used to be inhabited primarily by Jewish families, was empty, storefronts deserted.

"Father, remember when you said that you were treating Franz nicely for years for his protection, and then denied saying it? Did you think that something like this would ever happen to us, to necessitate his protection?"

"Well, in my worst nightmares I would never have dreamt of these terrible events happening in our country, in our town, to our people, or to our family. You must understand, son, it's always good to curry favors from rich and influential people. Especially for us Jews. You know some of our history, going back to biblical times, right? We've been persecuted before. We will always be persecuted. Nothing wrong with having extra protection."

Only after a week did we dare to venture outside.

That was an apocalypse-like afternoon. The sensation was weird and troubling. My friends were gone, and so were their families. Other people were living in their houses, operating their stores. We were now the outcasts. No one spoke to us. Everyone knew exactly who we were, why we were still in town, and how worthless and meaningless our lives had become, as we no longer owned the business that had shielded us.

After that, we lived like zombies. Avoiding human interaction, we only left home to get the minimum sun and exercise. Mother's Christian friends disappeared from our lives overnight.

"I'm sure Maria is now hosting a card game around our vintage Bavarian dining room set," she said cynically. "They were supposed to be our friends. No one raised a voice or made a cry on our behalf, when they placed our family and friends on the trains."

Both my parents lost weight and looked much older.

After a few weeks of pitiful existence, one morning I woke up to the sound of loud knocking. I already recognized Franz's assertive hand on our door. Father let him in. Mother and I were again on top of the staircase, listening carefully.

"Zoli, as of ten o'clock tomorrow morning, all White Certificates will officially become void. Your family will no longer be able to stay in Sečovce. I will no longer be able to protect you. I'm very sorry."

"Franz, you must help us. Where will we go?"

"They are now issuing Pink Certificates, to keep very few

essential Jews in Slovakia from deportation. But obtaining this certificate is above my pay grade and political contacts. You must believe me, I tried everything."

"Please, there must be something you can do to help us. Don't send us to the Nazis. You will be sending Irena, Alexander, and me to our death. We are friends!"

"I am so sorry, Zoli."

Franz paused and then spoke up again.

"There is one idea I was debating before coming here, which could potentially work. It's a long shot. Come and see me tomorrow first thing in the morning in my office. Having said that, you should also start preparing to leave. Please promise me you won't despair. Don't do anything stupid. This is not the end."

That insinuation reverberated throughout our space and was left hanging. We all knew what he was talking about.

The week before, my parents told me about two Jewish families that had been found dead in Košice the morning they were supposed to report to the train station for deportation. They decided to end their lives together, on their own terms. Parents and their children were found hanged. We did not speak of Franz's last words, but I know the three of us had the same thoughts on our minds.

Father left early the next day to see Franz.

In their meeting, he learned that the mayor was a close friend of the regional head of the *Garda*, a ruthless ground operator and organizer of violent gangs named Hudjka, whose office was located in nearby Michalovce. Within the *Garda*, Hudjka was responsible for handling all Jewish affairs in Eastern Slovakia. A few years before, Hudjka, a war-time profiteer and greedy person, initiated the opening of a luxurious and spacious religious bookstore that also sold stationery and office supplies, in Michalovce. He used the *Garda* team on the ground to promote the store and incentivize local residents to buy there. The store was named after the Saints Cyril and Methodius and managed by two old ladies, who apparently made it a habit to steal from the cash register. Hudjka was looking for a new, experienced, and more honest retail manager, and Franz suggested that he offer the position of manager to Father, who was skilled and seasoned. As Franz would explain to Hudjka, the seasoned Jewish trader would not only put the kibosh on theft but would also turn the Cyril and Methodius store into a gold mine of profits. Franz reiterated that there was no guarantee Hudjka would agree to this. Father thanked him and came back home.

We were sitting at home and listening to the debrief. Within 24 hours, we would learn whether we are to be delivered to the Nazis or become business associates with their collaborators, by partnering with the head of the local *Garda*.

The avaricious Hudjka accepted Franz's proposal without hesitation. He unquestionably loved money more than he loathed Jews.

That afternoon, Franz provided Father with a "temporary family pass" on a printed letter, explaining that "the Solomon Rosenberg case" was handled directly and personally by the esteemed Mr. Hudjka.

Two days later, our family was granted a Pink Certificate. Shortly thereafter, we left Sečovce and moved to Michalovce. We had very little time to pack our few remaining belongings, and even less food left to sustain us. I only took my two stamp albums and a few sets of clothes. I also made sure to pack the statue of the two French bulldogs that I kept.

Upon departure, our home was immediately confiscated by the *Garda*. As we stepped out, the three of us stopped and turned around for a last glance. Would we ever set foot in our house again?

Later that morning, we arrived at Michalovce by train and went into our small, rented flat, arranged by Hudjka's *Garda* squad.

Father reported immediately to Cyril and Methodius. Wasting no time and using a stamped letter of authorization signed by Hudjka, he laid off the two lady managers, and started recruiting and training a new sales team. The business started doing better almost instantaneously.

Hudjka was pleased to see the cash flowing again, and we were protected again.

The *Garda* boss would not agree to be publicly seen with a Jew. They never spoke directly or met. Instead, Hudjka showed his appreciation to Father by sending random monetary gifts and messages, conveyed to Father by one of the boss's henchmen.

There were a few other Jews left in Michalovce, and we kept in close contact with some of them. We made sure to always meet indoors, and kept very quiet, not to draw any unnecessary attention. These meetings were our only means of keeping abreast of war news and developments. People were already talking about concentration camps, forced labor camps, death camps in Poland, German and Slovak death squads, and unmentionable human grief and tragedies that had hit Slovak Jews. Despite our efforts, we couldn't get any news about my parents' siblings and other family members.

In those meetings, we learned more about our nemesis, the German *Schutzstaffel* (SS) [Protection Squadron]. Led by Heinrich Himmler, this paramilitary organization grew to become the monstrous orchestrator and executor of security, surveillance, and terror all over German-occupied Europe. The SS had three main parts. There was the Allgemeine SS [General SS], the enforcer of the Nazis' racial policies. There was the *Waffen-SS* [Armed SS], with combat units within Germany's military. And then, there was the *SS-Totenkopfverbände* [SS-Death Head units], which ran the concentration camps and extermination camps. This devilish establishment also included the Gestapo and the *Sicherheitsdienst* secret agencies, the most dreaded groups within the Nazi regime. All these people were out to get us.

It was now late 1943. Every Jew, half-Jew, or a person with "questionable" biological roots that might link them to Judaism, was to be reported, arrested, and deported from Slovakia, unless they were officially protected. Our family had now been serving time in a comfortable, protected confinement, for a third consecutive year.

"Father, tell me about your brothers who left for America."

"Well, a few years ago I wouldn't tell you I envied them. But now I do. Alexander and Simon are seven and five years older than I am, respectively. They live in Cleveland. Their state is called Ohio. Lawrence is two years younger than me. He lives in Los Angeles, on the West Coast, in a state called California. They all have salaried jobs and families. I haven't heard from any one of them for years now, since the post office stopped delivering the mail. Growing up, I loved them all, and we were close. I really hope we get a chance to meet them and their families someday."

"Why did they choose to leave Czechoslovakia in the first place? Did they predict that Jews would be persecuted?"

"I don't think anyone could have predicted this war. As for your first question, you will have to ask them that yourself. I guess they didn't see themselves as retail traders or store owners. Also, I guess they wanted a better economic opportunity. The world outside Czechoslovakia is wide and vast, and America has built a reputation for being the land of opportunity. They were more adventurous than I ever was, and simply wanted to explore."

"I really hope to visit them someday."

And then, a few weeks later, and seemingly out of nowhere, a *Garda* messenger showed up in our apartment with a brief message from Hudjka.

"He wishes to thank you for your good and loyal services, but they are no longer required. Effective immediately, your presence at the store is no longer needed."

"This can't be true, there is a lot of work at the business. I am training the new team. He just sent me a message last week to congratulate the team on last month's performance. Can I speak with him please?" Father was caught completely off guard.

"He does not want to send you and your family to the camps... but you have to disappear immediately. There is no more protection for any Jew in Slovakia. He asked me to give you this. He wishes you nothing but the best of luck."

The man handed over a sealed document envelope to my father and left.

He quickly opened the paper bag.

Hudjka's farewell gift consisted of three blank and signed official identity forms, three blank and signed birth certificates, and one blank and signed wedding certificate. Our life was undoubtedly interesting.

4 BRATISLAVA I

Sitting around the kitchen table, we took inventory. We had little money, a treasured packet of blank government papers, and a prompt eviction notice. We had to leave Michalovce within hours.

My parents had no clue what to do next. They were too emotionally drained to think this through, or play out our options, and my vote didn't really count yet. Should we go to Košice, trying our luck hiding in a larger city my parents knew well, where there would be people we could reach out to for help? Were these family members and friends still there, or had they been deported? Would we be better off escaping to the Tatri mountains and joining the fighting partisans? Could we physically withstand that? Do we travel to Bratislava, the lion's den, and seek contacts who had gone underground there?

The only family members we knew to be alive were my grandmother Theresa Rosenbaum and my mother's sisters Gisella and Elizabeth (Lizi). They were all hiding in Bratislava, the capital. Grandmother and Gisella were laying low under false identities, and we had their address. Lizi was living on the other side of the city with her husband, Ernst (Erno) Gallan.

Mother made the call. We were to leave for Bratislava immediately, on the first train out, to stay with her mother and youngest sister. She was very anxious about risking her family by seeking them out but determined that this option was probably the least bad, overall.

Then began a peculiar ritual, one in which we had to pick and agree on our new identities. Father had to come up with a new given name as sticking to 'Solomon' was out of the question. 'Irena' and 'Alexander' would pass as proper gentile names, so we got to keep them. We were looking for a family name that would be recognized as a common, non-Jewish peasant name typical of the region, not easily linkable to Rosenberg. By the end of the evening, we were Stefan Ružiak, Irena Ružiak, and Alexander Ružiak.

Father filled the birth certificates, the marriage certificate, and personal identification papers with the new details. We packed that night and didn't really sleep, anxiously awaiting sunrise. He allowed me to put my stamp collection and statue of the two French bulldogs in the suitcase.

Unbeknownst to us, around the same time we planned to travel westbound, the notorious SS officer Alois Brunner, Adolf Eichmann's loyal executor, arrived in Bratislava. His mission was to help the local, friendly regime finish off the remaining Jewish community of Slovakia. He was to focus resources and strategy towards capturing the hidden Jews. That included operating a wide net of intelligence officers and informers, interrogating captured refugees, documenting their methods of operation, and issuing orders to field units based on information gathered from interrogations.

Morning came.

Without saying a word to anyone, we boarded the first morning train to Bratislava as the Ružiak family, carrying our few valuables.

We were heading to the new nation's capital. I had never visited a metropolis before and was looking forward to exploring and appreciating the architecture and famous open markets. Those were such nice thoughts to calm down my anxieties.

The train ride was uneventful. Our car was filled with families and suitcases, and we definitely didn't stand out. I was examining the other passengers closely, to see if I could identify Jews on the run, like us.

"Do you think some of them are also Jews that are sitting in the gentile car under false identities?" I asked in a low voice.

Hearing my question, Mother almost suffered a heart attack. She held my arm firmly and shouted a whisper in my ear.

"Sanyi, get yourself together. This is not a game. We are one step removed from being captured, tortured, and killed. All it takes is one informant to alert an official that we are acting in a weird manner or looking a tad suspicious. Once they check our names and see that our documents were falsified, that will be the end of the three of us. You are an adult now, 16 years old. You are smart and careful. You have a responsibility to yourself and towards your father and me. Look around you. Remember that everyone around you is an informant. They will sell us out to the Gestapo for a bowl of soup, or a slice of bread, in a heartbeat. You are Alexander Ružiak now. No more of this Jew talk. Prove that we can trust you."

I felt deeply ashamed, my heart beating fast and mouth dry. Hugging her, I whispered back my apology and commitment to act intelligently and responsibly going forward.

When we arrived at the station in Bratislava, Father asked the train clerk for directions to my grandmother's apartment. We walked for almost an hour carrying our suitcases. We didn't stand out because the city streets were swarming with families, dragging crying toddlers, rushing, and carrying suitcases around. There were refugees everywhere.

Finally, we arrived at the hideout address. The street was quiet and empty. We carefully entered the foyer, making sure our luggage doesn't touch the ground to avoid making noises, looking out for curious neighbors, but saw no one. We climbed to the second floor, and Mother knocked gently on the door.

"Yes, who is that?"

"It's Irena."

The door opened slowly, and we were swiftly and firmly pulled inside. Once the door was shut and locked, Gisella, her finger on her mouth as to signal for silence, jumped and hugged her older sister in an audio-muted display of affection. She was just nine years older than I was.

"Never utter a word outside these four walls, and always speak quietly. In this city, in this neighborhood, in this building, all the walls have ears." Gisella made sure again the door was locked.

Grandmother Theresa was sitting in the living room, using a handkerchief to dry tears of joy in her eyes. Her oldest daughter went to her and held her hands. They didn't hug.

"Thank God, you're alive. It's been a month since we got your last letter, and we feared the worst. They renewed the deportations from the Košice area, you know," said Grandmother. She held me tight and wouldn't let go. I was so happy to see her after so many years. The exciting, chatty woman I used to spend my summers with was now an old, gray, and wrinkled shadow of her former self.

For fear of the secret police, Grandmother and Aunt Gisella never revealed any details of their escape from Trebišov in the letters they sent us. Mother's brother Bella managed to obtain falsified papers for them and for his girlfriend Ilonka and brought the three of them to this small one-bedroom apartment, before disappearing in the mountains to join the Russian partisans in their brave fight against the German Army.

"We had to flee Michalovce when we learned we were no longer protected. It all happened very fast. Now we have nowhere to go. Can we stay here with you for a few days until Zoli finds a place for us to stay?" asked Mother, her voice cracking.

"Of course, my child. The place is small, but you can stay for as long as you need to." Tears were running down Grandmother's face and she kept drying them with her handkerchief. "But we will all have to be very careful. There is a neighbor on the ground floor who is a Gestapo snitch. He reports on anyone coming in or leaving the building. Thankfully, I believe he is at his factory shift now, like during most mornings. Did anyone see you entering the building?"

"I don't know," Father answered. "I don't think so. How do we manage to keep our presence here a secret from this neighbor?"

"I know this man's work schedule. We need to make sure that Zoli is the only person going in or out, as needed. Otherwise, you must all stay here, quietly."

The place was tiny for six people, but we had no real alternative. In the morning, Gisella would leave first to make sure the entrance was clear. If she stomped her foot twice, Father knew it was safe for him to leave. They both had a set meeting time outside the building in the evening. If Gisella stood at the entrance, that meant it was safe for him to return to the apartment. If she didn't, he was to come back around the block every 60 minutes to see if the coast was clear.

During the day, we had nothing to do and hence plenty of time to reflect on our predicament.

"Mother, when was the last time you heard from your friends in Sečovce?"

"What friends are you referring to?"

"Maria and Katarina."

She didn't answer at first. Her face was expressionless, but her voice gave away a touch of sadness. She almost never cried.

"I don't have friends anymore. Maria and Katarina were never my true friends. I only have the both of you, and our family here."

"But they were your friends before the war. You always explained how important it was to make close friends like the ones you had. Why would you say that you had no friends?"

"Having friends is the most wonderful thing. We did have good times together for many years. But it turned out they were not true friends. They didn't lift a finger to protect us, or to protest what was happening to us. When being my friend came at a cost, or posed a risk to them, they showed their real faces."

"I'm sorry. I hope you find real friends. All my friends from school went on the train that morning back home. I hope they are back so I could see them sometime."

"I hope so too, Sanyi."

After a week of walking the streets and looking for "for rent" signs, Father found an apartment we could lease at the heart of the elegant neighborhood of Červená, situated on one of the city's highest hills, and somewhat distant from the city center.

To protect our family's safety, we agreed on a regular weekend meeting place with Grandmother and Gisella on one of the bridges over the Danube River.

"Can I leave this with you for safe keeping?" I asked Gisella, handing over the metal statue of the two French bulldogs. "I have a sense they are better off staying in this apartment, than going with us."

Gisella laughed and took the statue. "Only for safe keeping! You must promise to pick the statue up after the war."

"I promise!"

Our new apartment was located on the ground floor of an old brick house. Half of it was buried below street level. Our landlady Marika seemed nice and friendly and wore fancy dresses and heavy makeup. Marika liked sharing information about herself. Her boyfriend was a Captain in the *Wehrmacht*, fighting the Russians on the Eastern Front. He visited her every few weeks and we chatted with him when he spent time there, listening to stories of German bravery in battles of tanks and armored units against the "barbaric" Red Army.

Marika never suspected that we were Jews. Our German was perfect, and we each looked our Christian part. Our cover story, which Father built meticulously, was that we had been running away from the Eastern Front, deeply fearing a Bolshevik occupation.

Mother and Marika gradually became close, finding numerous cultural bridges, ranging from Hungarian opera to Prussian literature. We were settling down in our new, invented lives. I was no longer obsessed with, or haunted by, the fear of getting caught and deported to the Nazi extermination camps.

"Alexander, did you have a girlfriend back home in the east?" asked Marika while serving us fresh mint tea. "I'm sure you did, a handsome fellow like yourself."

My parents looked at me with interest and amusement. Yet another taboo topic that was never discussed at home.

"No. I was always too busy with my apprenticeship and schoolwork," I answered. "Didn't have time for girls, unfortunately."

"A handsome, tall, and strong young man like you, I'm sure you'll find a nice girl here in Bratislava and settle down. Church is the best place for that. What church did you say you belonged to back home?"

"Greek-Catholic," I answered without hesitation, sticking to our cover story.

"We haven't found a suitable congregation here in Bratislava yet," said Mother, coming to my rescue. "Obviously you are a Catholic, but would you know of a Greek-Catholic church in the neighborhood?"

"I will ask around on Sunday. Sometime ago I heard there was a nice Greek-Catholic church in Nové Mesto. You should probably check it out if you make it there."

"We sure will," said Mother. "Thank you."

I spent my days walking along the tree-lined streets, climbing up and down the hills, and carefully keeping away from the occasional military patrol. I was bored out of my mind, not having seen, or spoken to, a person my age for many long weeks. Applying to or being admitted to any school was out of the question, as we couldn't risk our papers being examined.

"Sanyi, you should start going out looking for a job," said Father over dinner. "I don't think you will raise any suspicion, as our identity here is now firm. The skills you developed during your apprenticeship would allow you to become an assistant typewriter technician."

"Are you sure I can handle that job?"

"Yes. You have such good hands. We are getting short on money, and Mother and I can see you are already climbing the walls with boredom. I've mapped a number of typewriter businesses in the commercial district that you should visit to see if they have openings."

He was right.

The first place I visited the next morning, a Mercedes typewriter agency named Miloslav Schweska, was desperately looking for junior apprentices. Pay was modest, but fair, and the owner treated me nicely. My cover story was not challenged and over my months there I became an integral part of the team.

In spite of all his efforts, Father couldn't land a job; he spent his days wandering the streets and avenues, knocking on retail doors to discuss openings, unsuccessfully.

"How was your day, Zoli? Any luck finding a position?" She asked every night, even though she already knew the answer.

"Nothing," he answered every day.

He grew gloomy and tired, and I didn't know what to do to cheer him up. I was getting worried about him.

Mother and I should have read his signs of desperation, the weakening of his instincts. We should have been proactive and reassured him, taking the immense pressure of providing off of his shoulders. Succumbing to our own fatigue and emotional numbness, we didn't read the writing on the wall. And the consequences were detrimental and dire.

"How was your day, Zoli? Any luck finding a position?" she asked during dinner.

"No, but you won't believe what happened to me today. Do you remember Dov Schwartz? Out of all the people in the world, we bumped into each other today, just across from Michalská brána."

Mom's forehead furrowed. "And? What is Schwartz doing in the city? How was he not deported?"

"He was obviously shocked to see me in Bratislava. Such a blessing to come across an old acquaintance from back home. You won't believe the terrible things he told me about his nephew's family. You remember Ezekiel, right? Terrible, terrible story. We spoke about getting together to catch up."

I could tell her senses were on high alert. Alarms went off in her head.

"I hope you didn't provide him with any details about our new identity or any information about our whereabouts. I don't need to remind you, but informers come in all shapes and forms. There are many Jewish informants. We shouldn't trust anyone who's not an immediate family member." Her eyes were staring at Father. She wasn't blinking.

"You shouldn't worry about Dov. He is a good man, most definitely not an informer. We've known him since childhood. Don't be ridiculous."

"Did you, or did you not, share our home address with him?"

"I did, but don't get worked out about it. He is in hiding with his family as well, and we needed a meeting place away from town center. He really wanted to see you and Sanyi. It will be great to meet a dear old friend together."

"I can't believe you did that. Promise me – no, swear to me – that you will never again give away our location to anybody else."

"I promise, dear. Again, nothing to be concerned about."

It didn't matter anymore.

The next day, a gray and wet afternoon of October 1944, a small company of German soldiers arrived in an open military truck on our street, stopped in front of our house, and broke into our apartment with pointed rifles. I had just walked in from work. Both my parents were home.

"Ružiak?" they asked.

They didn't wait for any of us to respond. "Jewish pigs, we know that your real name is Rosenberg. The charade is over, you are coming with us now."

We were shocked. Mother looked at Father but said nothing.

"There must be a mistake, sir. Our name is Ružiak. Please, check our papers. You can also speak with our landlord, she will confirm our identity," said Father pleadingly.

The full-bodied corporal landed his gun's butt forcefully into Father's abdomen, who fell down in agony.

"Silence, Jew. I don't need to examine your fake papers. The three of you are coming with us."

Father fell into Schwartz's trap and led the Gestapo hunters directly to our hiding place. Schwartz was a Jewish informer. To save his skin and protect his family, he roamed the streets of Bratislava, keeping both eyes open for Jews who were hiding in the city under assumed identities.

I helped him get back on his feet.

Years of careful planning and execution, a lifetime and fortune spent on acquiring protection at the highest levels, a solid hiding plan, all lost in one moment of weakness.

The soldiers allowed us to pack and bring along one suitcase. There was not a lot left anyway, except for my mother's gold bracelet and Persian fur, which she still managed to hold on to as our emergency hard assets. Both items were already carefully hidden inside the suitcase in preparation for a quick exit scenario, and the soldiers couldn't see them. One of the Germans saw my only treasured item, the two stamp albums, and put them under his arm. How proud I was of that collection, now lost forever. I couldn't help but think about the lucky French bulldogs, who were safely resting in the hands of Gisella.

We were pushed into the truck that started driving towards the center of Bratislava. Father looked defeated, his face showing no expression. Mother's eyes were fixated on the canvas ceiling, her teeth clenched. I couldn't fathom his naivete. That's what she had complained about all these years.

The truck stopped outside an exceptionally wide house on Kozia Street. There were armed Slovak guards outside and a swastika flag hanging out of the first-floor balcony. Inside, it looked like a makeshift deportation station.

On the entrance floor we passed through a number of desks, manned by five clerks surrounded by mountains of papers, stamps, typewriters, and armed soldiers. Our captors led us into a large hall on the second floor and asked that we stay there. We found ourselves in the company of men, women, children, and many suitcases. It smelled like walking into an old person's closet. Most of the people were lying on their coats, spread on the wooden floor. We were obviously not the only Jewish family hiding in Bratislava and eventually captured. There was a large-scale, citywide hunt going on, and all of us there got caught. I wondered which of the other families were also Schwartz's victims. We heard and shared grim stories and speculations of things to come.

The heating system was not operating, and the room was freezing cold. There were no blankets or mattresses. Our jailers offered only dry bread and water, mornings, and evenings. We slept on the floor, using our luggage and a few belongings as pillows. There were no bathrooms.

Disgusted by his misjudgment and fateful mistake, Father seemed beaten. He barely spoke to us during our first day there and wouldn't look us in the eye. He spent time with a few of the men who were sitting close to us.

"I will fix this, Irena," he whispered that evening. "It's all my fault, and I will fix it."

"Don't be stupid, Zoli. There's nothing you can do now. The damage is done. You'll just get yourself killed."

"Don't worry, I have a plan."

"Please, promise me you don't do anything stupid."

"Mr. Weiss, the person standing behind us, told me that the senior civilian clerk in this command post downstairs is taking bribes. He told me another family left last week after paying him off. I know what I'm doing. That's our only chance to save ourselves. We won't have another one."

"Yesterday you believed Schwartz, and now we find ourselves

here. Now you want to believe Weiss? Will you ever learn not to believe or put your trust in people you don't know?"

"That's enough. I made a mistake and I wish I could turn back the clock. I can't do that. We can only look forward, and this is what we must do." He turned away.

Without further delay, he reached his hand into the suitcase, grabbed the bracelet and Persian fur from the hidden compartment, and quietly climbed down the stairs to seek the crooked clerk. He walked up the stairs five minutes later in measured steps, his hands empty.

"What happened?", she whispered.

"He took them, the weasel," he whispered back.

"What now?"

"Now we wait."

The Rosenbergs were now out of hard currency.

We fell asleep on the floor.

Deafening shouting and army boots banging on the wooden floors woke us up early the next morning.

A soldier was standing at the end of the hall, loudly commanding everyone to orderly vacate the second-floor hall, exit out to the street, and form lines of three.

The three of us formed a single line in the middle of the human pack on the paved road. I stood closest to the curbside. Soldiers and clerks marched up and down, counting attendees, making notes, and comparing their lists.

Out of nowhere, one of the clerks approached us and brutally kicked my behind. "You scoundrels, what business do you have here with the filthy Jews? Get lost!" he shouted.

Looking at Father, it was apparent that my buttocks were harmed by the current owner of Mother's bracelet and fur, the weasel. Had Father actually managed to save us?

We immediately excused ourselves and started walking away without looking back. No one followed us. They let us go. Leaving the deportee parade together with us was the Weiss family, who had most likely also gifted our benefactor handsomely.

The rest of the group began marching down the street towards the train station, accompanied by the soldiers. We walked quickly in the opposite direction, northbound. Mr. Weiss and his family slowly disappeared into an alley, and we never saw them again.

Free once more and without a penny in our pockets, we entered a small community park and sat on a bench. We must have looked like the sole survivors of an epic plane crash or earthquake, pale, shivering, and shocked. The insanely fast turn of events was overwhelming even for the rugged fugitives we'd become.

"What do we do now?" I asked.

"We can't go to my mother's place," she said. "If we are being followed, we will expose them and get them captured."

"We don't have any money," said Father. "And we can't stay here in the park or out on the street. Within minutes, a patrol will stop us for questioning and ask for our papers. We must stay off the streets, go back to our apartment, and hope the weasel keeps his mouth shut, and no one learns of this."

The idea of going back to the place of our capture gave me chills, but there really was no other alternative.

Marika was staring out the window as we were approaching her front door. She ran out to greet us, her yelling reverberated across the neighborhood. "Blessed Jesus! Blessed God! Blessed, kind Virgin Mary! I knew that the stupid Germans made a terrible mistake. How could they do this to you?"

"Thank you, my dear friend, what would we do without you," said Mother as she hugged her. "Can you believe the nerve of these people? They think they can do whatever they want to a good Christian family, just because they have guns and uniforms. We are famished. Would you have anything for us to snack on until I can fix my family a meal?"

"Of course, you poor creatures, come in! I mean, how can anyone in their right mind mistake a pure Aryan family such as yourselves for filthy Jews?"

"Ask the Germans," said Mother. "Beats me."

"The bastards! I want to hear all about what you had to go through... I'm really aching for you. As you know, my boyfriend is a senior officer in the German Army. He will make sure heads will roll over this. It's just not right!"

We sat down to have potatoes and cabbage with Marika. She also gave Mother some money so we could buy food.

We had to play the game as if nothing had happened, beyond an unfortunate mistake. That same afternoon, I went back to Miloslav Schweska to explain my absence and see if I could get my old job back. Unfortunately, they could not hire me back as business was spiraling downwards. The Eastern Front was edging ever closer to Bratislava, residents were leaving the city, and commerce was being pounded.

"I'm proud of you, Zoli," I heard her tell him. "You saved us. I'm sorry I was so upset with you and for doubting you."

"We are not out of the woods yet," he answered. "If we had any money, I would leave this location at once. They can come for us at any time."

Days went by and we started hoping that we were safe.

It took the Gestapo three weeks to the day. A taxi stopped in front of our house one morning. An SS officer, dressed in civilian clothes, knocked on our door. We were all at home.

"Mr. Rosenberg, Mrs. Rosenberg, young Mr. Rosenberg," said the German, "spare me the wide eyes, we know everything."

Our streak of luck had finally run its course. We had been lucky for almost five years, playing cat and mouse with the Germans.

"We know that you are Jews, we know about the false papers, we also know about the fine necklace and the expensive fur. That stupid clerk is in our custody, he will go on trial and eventually be shot. Pack your things, you are coming with me."

Without saying a word, we went into the back seat of the taxi with our suitcase. The officer sat up front next to the driver, and we drove back to the Gestapo roundup house downtown.

There was no way out for us this time, no bribable weasel to scoop us out of a lineup.

After spending three days in the same large, second-floor hall, alongside newly captured Jewish families, we experienced the déjà vu of waking up at dawn to the loud voice of the same rowdy soldier. We hurried outside and stood orderly in lines of three.

The German soldiers walked us to the train station.

The train we boarded delivered us to a transfer camp called Nováky. We spent two days under a large tent waiting for another train to take us to our next destination.

While preparing to exit the camp, men and women were being separated. When ordered to board the train, I was put together in a group with Father, and Mother was taken to a different car.

"I love you, Mother, take care of yourself! We will meet soon in Bratislava, in your sister's house," I shouted as she walked away from us to the other side of the track. The three of us had remained closely together while in hiding over the last three years, and I wasn't ready to let her go.

"Take care of him, he needs you," she answered in a high-pitched voice.

"I promise," I answered, but my voice was swallowed in a cacophony of screams, and Mother was no longer in sight.

We both boarded the cattle car with hundreds of other men.

"Hold my hand tight, Sanyi. We must stick together."

I held on to him as hard as I could. The human hive pulled and pushed us into one of the corners of the car. We knew nothing about our destination. We didn't know where Mother was being taken to.

The train started moving.

We were heading north, out of Slovakia. I had never left my birth country before that night. No passport was required for this journey.

5 IN THE CAMP

The four-day train ride was hell on earth. The nightmares I kept
having about my friends from Sečovce, rounded up, marched, and
transferred on board a train to Poland, paled in comparison to the
jarring reality.

We were a human mash of hundreds. We could barely move.
Father and I were firmly compressed one against each other, chest to
chest. Seventeen years with Father, I'd never felt his body this close
to mine. At least a dozen other men were applying pressure on my
body, my leg muscles straining and pumping to support a stable
position. We still had our small suitcase at our feet, with some food
and a few articles of clothing in it.

It was hard to breathe. The mixed stench of feces, sweat, dirty
clothes, and urine combined with the body odor of mules and cows,
most likely the regular cargo in that car. As a sole means of
ventilation, the compartment had a single, tiny, barred window. Each
car had been allocated a large steel bucket so passengers could relieve
themselves. It got filled up after a few hours and there was nowhere
to empty it. The stench was so great that people were throwing up
everywhere.

Early during the trip, people were whispering, silently speaking in German, Russian, Hungarian, Polish, Czech, Slovak, and Yiddish all around us.

"Do you know where the train is headed?"

"Do you have a piece of bread you could spare? God bless you."

"I can barely breath, I'm asthmatic, could you please give me some more room?"

"You are hurting my hand, please step back."

"I need to go urgently, I'm suffering from a condition, let me get to the corner of the car, please clear the way!"

"Do you know Lipa Horowitz? Is he on the train? When did you last see him in Bratislava?"

The train kept going.

The person who was compressed against the window would describe in German what he saw to the other passengers, offering his own interpretations and thoughts.

"Train signs and road signs are now all in German. We must have entered Germany."

"Massive destruction in this city, it's still smoky. The old cathedral is destroyed. Must have been a recent air raid by the Allied Forces. Horses running free everywhere. Dead bodies on the ground next to the railway."

"Three tanks and a few armored vehicles heading in the opposite direction. They carry Waffen-SS marks."

"Army roadblock with soldiers on motorcycles. Checking papers of people in their cars. A long cue stretching as far as the eye can see."

Occasionally, we heard the noise of a man dropping to the ground. Several older and weaker fellow travelers couldn't hold on. Their bodies collapsed unceremoniously. After they fell, dead, their neighbors would drag them to one of the corners of the car.

Two or three times a day, the train stopped at a station, and the person by the window who had the best view would report the activities taking place outside.

"A line of prisoners is being led to the back of the train. They are boarding one of the cars. Only young men."

"German soldiers debarked. They are entering the office."

"Prisoners are carrying large boxes to the adjacent car."

Every other station, the car door would open, and the sunlight blinded us. Two or more soldiers outside would point their guns at the car. "You," they said, pointing at a random prisoner, "bring the bucket of shit and climb down to empty it on the track."

I was volunteered to empty the bucket during one of these stops. My legs were numb, and I almost crashed face down, trying to climb out from the car. A large sign on top of the passenger terminal spelled "Dresden."

"There are a few dead men in the car. May we take out their bodies?" I dared to ask.

"Shut up and climb back to the car with the bucket."

I picked up the empty bucket and climbed up.

For many of the hours, days, and nights we were clenched together, I was thinking of Father. For so long he had been an undisputed community and business leader, head of a family, gifted salesman, and affluent property owner; now he was reduced to a stinking nothing, caged among many dozens of fellow sticking nothings. He never liked sharing his thoughts, so I attempted to read them. I needed to know he was not going to give up, because it occurred to me how easy it would be to decide on giving up, back there and then, in the train cattle car.

"Are you okay?" I whispered.

"I'm okay, Sanyi. Are you okay?"

"Yes. We are together, right? To the bitter end, right?"

"We are, Sanyi."

It gradually became more spacious, as we were losing passengers by the hour. Their bodies were now a human pile of dead. We had more space to stretch our legs and sit down. I put my head on Father and fell asleep. After I woke up, it occurred to me that my nightmare was still surrounding me, and tears started rolling down my cheeks. I covered my face and dried them up.

On the fourth night, the train arrived at its final station. The door opened and a company of soldiers was staring into the reeking car.

"Quickly, everybody must exit the train at once!" shouted one of them.

"Form a single line parallel to the car! Quickly!"

"Forward march!"

Everyone jumped out, carrying their few belongings. Everyone but the dead. There were at least 30 bodies lying in piles at the corners of the car. They were old and thin. Glancing at their motionless corpses and blank facial expressions while climbing down from the car, I felt mixed emotions about their death. In some ways, they were the lucky ones.

We knew that we had just disembarked somewhere in the heart of the Third Reich, in northern Germany, but had no idea where exactly.

The night air was freezing with powerful wind gusts, carrying flurries of old snowflakes from trees and building roofs in the station. Gravely underdressed, we were both shivering as we marched on. The long line of prisoner-refugees walked from the train station through a large, admonitory entrance gate with clear German letter signage. We had arrived at the Sachsenhausen Concentration Camp, in the outskirts of the capital.

Mother, I made it to Berlin! Or at least to a suburb of Berlin. I always pictured our Bar Mitzvah family trip to Berlin with bright colors and glitzy outfits. I expected wide, tree-lined avenues, fancy cafes, haute cuisine, celebratory steak, chocolate truffles, and designer shoe stores. Instead, I was surrounded by death and disease, while parading alongside a miserable crowd on a frosty, dark night.

The soldiers led us to an immense roundup ground at the center of the camp. They ordered us to arrange in neat lines, each comprising a few dozen men, and made sure the lines were parallel and orderly. We waited there for almost a day and half. People around were literally falling off their tired feet. During daytime, every time a man fell, a soldier would swiftly appear and shout at them to stand back up.

For the first time, I saw, in addition to the SS staff and army soldiers, people wearing prisoner clothes with cloth bands around their arms, walking freely around the camp, interacting with the German personnel, and ordering prisoners around.

"Who are these people? Are they not prisoners like us?" I asked Father.

"I don't know," he answered.

"Those are the Kapos," said a person who stood next to Father in Yiddish. "I heard about them from my neighbor who spent months in a labor camp. The Germans are short of manpower, so they earmark and cherry pick trustworthy prisoners to do their dirty job for them. The Kapos get extra food and better lodging for that. I spit on them! Curse them all! Stinking traitors."

Kapos came and left, speaking with the soldiers. In the morning of the second day, Kapos started carrying away all the suitcases and bags that were brought by the men on the train. We labored so hard to save that valise during our trip here, only to see it being carried away by a Kapo. Father and I were left with the thin clothes and light coats on our bodies.

"Hey, you!" one of the Kapos addressed me, after he saw the Doxa watch flashing on my wrist. "I'll take that now."

I looked at Father and took the watch off. In the grand scheme of life's swift, meteoric collapse, losing a watch felt quite meaningless.

"Where you're going, young man, you won't be needing this," the Kapo smiled sardonically, grabbed the watch, and left.

Where were we going? I had a flash of an amusing thought of us all heading for a swim at the lake but knew that the Kapo had something very different in mind.

On the evening of the second day, a group of soldiers arrived. One of them ordered only the left part of our group, where we were standing, to form tidy marching rows, and started leading us in the same direction we came from originally. We were about 80 people, accompanied by six soldiers and their barking dogs.

We marched away from the roundup area, out through the main gate, and onto the main road. From there, we crossed to an unpaved, muddy path, covered with deep snow and a frozen top layer of ice. It became harder and harder to walk.

After about three hours of plodding, I felt a firm German hand gripping my shoulder. "Outside, now," he shouted. "Do you speak German?"

I nodded my head up and down.

It was pitch dark, probably well after midnight. Nocturnal animals, birds, and mammals were chirping and growling in the shadows. There was no doubt in my mind that this well-fed, tall Aryan beast was going to kill me, and my heart was beating fast. He ordered me to follow him. We walked to the side of the road and when we stopped, the marching group was already almost out of sight.

"Boy, do you see that old man lying in the ditch behind?" he barked in German. "Run there, pick him up, carry him, and return to the group at once. If you try something funny you will be shot immediately."

Relieved, I ran back to pick up the old man. The poor creature was supine, groaning and weeping on the snowy mud. I reached out my hands and lifted his very light body, easily placing him on my shoulder, and progressed in fast steps to catch up with the group. The tall soldier kept a close eye and a small distance, walking behind us. The three of us promptly caught up with the line of prisoners, and I continued carrying the old man for another few hours. His weeping was replaced by subtle silent sighs that felt synchronized with the pace of my steps. I carefully listened to them, making sure he was breathing.

At the break of dawn, we arrived at a small, run-down airfield in the outskirts of the town of Oranienburg. According to tumbledown signage there, the airfield was part of a Heinkel aircraft factory, almost completely demolished by air bombings.

We marched into a half-flattened hangar that reminded me of a scene from an apocalyptic, German fiction book I had read in the early days of the war. Most of its roof was missing, and there was debris everywhere. The part of the hangar that remained standing was converted into an ad hoc prisoner camp, probably because other regional compounds were completely full, overflowing with pathetic, former humans like us. We saw other inmates there, most of them looking thin, pale, and frail. We were allocated bunk beds and veteran prisoners served us a meal for the first time since our arrival to Germany. Each of us received a small metal bowl containing lukewarm watery soup and a few small colorless potatoes floating in it.

I sat down on my bunk bed and started carefully peeling the potatoes, discarding the peels onto the floor, planning to carry those peels over to the trash canister when I was done eating. Unbeknownst to me, I was being watched closely by other inmates, hungry and exhausted. No sooner had the last peel touched the floor than they jumped manically towards me and went for the potato peels. Mayhem broke out, and two pitiful blokes practically tried to kill each other over my peels. Another reality check. I learned to never, ever discard a potato peel, or any other vegetable peel, or anything edible, again, because no calorie was insignificant to a prisoner.

That night, I slept a few hours horizontally for the first time in many days.

In the morning they took away our clothes during roll call. It was the first time I saw Father completely naked. I didn't think much of it, because I was cold and hungry.

We were ordered, along with a group of about 200 other prisoners, to enter a large shower room deeper inside the hangar. The room had wide metallic water sprinklers hanging from the ceiling. Before pumping in the water, a group of soldiers entered, carrying long industrial brushes. They smeared all of us with disinfecting soap and anti-lice cream and put the brushes to aggressive use. They scraped us ear to toe using the hard, metallic brushes. It was the most painful experience I had ever known. Once they left, boiling water started flowing out of the shower caps and burnt our bodies. Everyone was screaming from pain, but fortunately the ordeal lasted less than 30 seconds. After leaving the room and going out into the wintry freezing weather, each of us was allowed to pick up a small piece of cloth to dry our bodies. We were then placed on the line awaiting the barber. He shaved off all my hair with an electric shaver.

We were then handed new prisoner clothes. Very briskly, everyone was given a shirt, a pair of pants, wooden-soled shoes, and a flannel strap to protect and warm our kidneys.

"Bloody Germans. They are being scientific even when torturing and enslaving us," muttered Father.

"What do you mean?" I asked.

He was too exhausted to answer. He was probably as surprised as I was about the flannel straps. It was a smart and inexpensive way to protect the critical organs of forced laborers in the freezing German winter.

The clothing articles were, for the most part, obviously in wrong sizes, and a fierce apparel and accessory exchange process ensued. Naked, tall prisoners holding on to child-sized pants and shirts were frantically seeking a swap, looking for shorter people who may have larger sizes to barter.

A well-dressed German civilian was standing at the epicenter of this spontaneous Turkish bazaar, shouting his lungs out. "Hurry up, maggots! Dress up quickly and move back into ranks."

He was holding onto a long wooden stick with a metal head, hitting people all around him to speed them up.

Luckily for us both, we received clothing articles of reasonable sizes. My shirt's sleeves were somewhat short, but I made the call not to risk an exchange debacle.

Disinfected, clean, shaven, and dressed in fresh uniforms, we received our personal identification number, which was attached to the front of the shirt. Daydreaming, I imagined that the scene was part of the end-of-year school diploma award ceremony, and it made me grin for a few seconds. Alas, there were no flowers, no emotional grandmothers, or celebratory pickled fish served on wooden tables in the church yard. Instead, we got a triangular-shaped identification sign to indicate our prisoner category. Our individual identification numbers were worn on top of the triangle.

Jews wore yellow triangles.

Gypsies wore brown ones.

Homosexuals wore pink.

Prisoners-of-war wore blue.

Those prisoners who were identified as *Bibelforscher* [Bible Scholars], mainly Jehovah's Witnesses, wore purple triangles.

The tag and number allocation ceremony only took a few minutes. When it was over, we were all placed in lines for another roundup.

We stayed in that hangar for a few more days, and my body felt weaker with each passing day, living off of the watery soup and the few floating potatoes. As days passed, I started eating the peels very quickly. On day three, the soldiers started roll call by calling out the names and separating the groups. Fewer prisoners remained in the hangar every day.

On day five, our names were called, along with those of a few hundred others. Minutes later, we were already marching to the closest train station in Oranienburg. An hour later, we boarded a cattle car, and the train started moving again.

It was déjà vu. We were in a part of a pack of smelly men again, with the people around us just thinner and younger than in the last time. I also didn't mind it as much as I did the first time.

This trip was much shorter than the one from Bratislava to Sachsenhausen. It only took a couple of days and didn't result in fatalities inside the car. The feeble and old were lucky to no longer be among us.

We arrived at a large station, with multiple parallel railway tracks funneling into it. The building was standing on an elevated plain. We disembarked. It was frostier than on any day we'd experienced in Germany thus far. Walking neatly in ranks, we soon entered through the iron gates of a wide brick building with a menacing clock tower in the middle.

JEDEM DAS SEINE read the German words on the gate.

"What do they mean by that?" I asked Father as we were keeping pace with the ranks. My mind couldn't connect the philosophical substance with the uninviting surroundings.

"It means they think they can turn us into forced laborers or slaughter us all with utter impunity. You will live to tell our story, Sanyi, be sure of that," he answered.

We arrived at the largest of all German concentration camps in World War II, Buchenwald, in the outskirts of Weimar, the former capital of the late Weimar Republic, terminally crushed under the Nazi Party boots. Most people referred to the camp as KLB, short for *Konzentrationslager Buchenwald*. I was looking around for beech trees (*Buchen*) or any type of forest (*Wald*), but all I could see were barbed wires, tents, large wooden blocks, numerous German uniforms, and the looming crematorium chimney, expelling white smoke all day and all night.

We marched through the gate, to the roundup area, joining a long line of prisoners who must have arrived on board of trains ahead of us. Civilian clerks registered the new arrivals, and we were all taken through another round of haircuts, this time without stripping naked. During the hours at the roundup, we heard from other prisoners about the Russian advances in the East, that the infamous Auschwitz extermination camp in Poland was about to be captured by the Red Army, and that consequently no more transports were heading its way. We understood that this was most likely the reason we were still alive, and now in Buchenwald. We debated whether the bribe handed by Father in Bratislava bought us the invaluable weeks that eliminated our terminal path to the gas chambers in Poland.

We were also told that Buchenwald, as expansive as it was, had been overcrowded for more than two years and currently was still beyond its full intake capacity. There was no way to crowd these new transports into the massive wooden barracks in the Main Camp.

To accommodate this overflow, the SS constructed an adjacent tent camp and called it *Kleineslager* [Small Camp]. We were assigned there, alongside what I estimated as at least 10,000 other new prisoners.

Our tents did not have beds, only tall wooden bunks, each with four levels of compartments, without mattresses or any form of padding. There was not nearly enough space in the bunks for all prisoners, so multiple inmates would cram together on each bunk to keep warm at night.

During the day, we were not allowed to stay in the tents and had to walk about in the cold snow with nothing to warm our bodies but our thin shirts and pants. For most daytime hours each day, more than 10,000 people would wander around in circles within the double barbed-wire fences of the Small Camp, trying to keep warm. We were only allowed to gather when waiting in food lines for meals.

Every late afternoon, the soldiers would conduct a final daily roundup in the center of the yard after which we were allowed to enter the tents.

On our first day, instantly after the soldiers released us, we saw that prisoners started a mad dash towards the tents. Father understood immediately, and said, "Run with me, quickly, don't let go of my hand."

Everyone wanted to be first in the tent in order to secure space on a bunk or the floor for the night. The bunks and tents could not accommodate all prisoners, and many of them, especially older and slower ones, didn't stand a chance of securing a space for themselves. The alternative, spending the night outdoors in the extreme cold, was a death sentence to many.

We made it into the tent that night, but just barely. As we huddled on a bunk bed with two other prisoners, I thought of the miserable others spending the night outside. How soon would it be for us spending the night outside in the freezing temperatures?

The next day, as we were walking together near the fence, Father stopped me while staring at a point near the fence.

I could sense his brain wheels turning.

"Sanyi, can you spot that thin wooden plank leaning against the nearest watchtower?"

"Yes." I looked at him and could barely identify the elegant, well-mannered, and proud business owner, who used to stand behind the Solomon Rosenberg counter, offering small talk, pralines, and Ceylon tea to his distinguished customers. In front of me was a rack of bones in a prisoner's suit. We were both debilitated and exhausted.

"Please run along and bring it back with you. Quickly, but try not to draw attention. I'll wait for you right here."

"Why would you want me to bring that thin wooden plank?"

"Just listen to what I tell you and hurry up. Stop asking questions."

I dashed and picked up the light plank. It was about three feet long, two feet wide, and very thin.

"From now on, everywhere you go, you take this plank with you. Did you hear me?"

"Yes." I didn't ask any more questions.

I could run very fast, but he couldn't. The fact that we were together eliminated any speed advantage I had over other prisoners. At night, disbursing from the roll call, I couldn't just run to find available bunk space, or he would be lost in the crowd and may be left out in the cold for the night.

"At the end of the roundup, hold my hand firmly and we will again run together," I told him.

During that evening roundup we ended up standing close to the farthest side of the prisoner formation. I was holding him with one hand and carrying the thin wooden plank with the other. By the time we arrived at the tent, the entrance had already been completely blocked by a pile of humans and we knew we couldn't make it inside. It was time to experience the quintessential KLB adventure: a night out in the wintery open air without any protection.

We walked away silently. The temperature was below freezing, and I was still beating myself up for not getting us into the tent in time to secure a spot. Luckily for us, the wind wasn't blowing at all that night.

"Listen to me, Sanyi. If we don't handle ourselves smartly in the coming hours, the cold will kill us. We must sleep, and at the same time we must make sure we don't freeze in the snow."

"How do we do that?"

"We will take shifts sleeping on the plank. The person awake will have to continuously rub the sleeping person's body, head to toe, so we both don't freeze. It's critically important that you don't fall asleep during your shift, or we will both turn to icicles."

I then understood why he insisted on securing and protecting the wooden plank. His plan sounded completely insane to me, but I couldn't think of a better one. We identified a corner in the yard where snow was partly shoveled, and the ground was less rocky and placed the plank down on the wet soil, after making sure it was stable.

Not far from us stood a small group of Orthodox Jews who were also left outside the tent for the night. Their hair had been shaved off, and they were loudly reciting Psalms in Hebrew. Father approached one of them using his perfect Yiddish.

"Good evening, sir."

No response.

"Good evening, sir, my name is Zoli Rosenberg. It's going to be a very cold night. It will be dangerous for all of you because you can freeze out here. Would you like to share the sleeping plank and sleep shifts with us? Two can sleep on the plank, sharing body heat, and the third one would rub their bodies to keep them warm. We will all benefit from partnering."

"No, thank you, Mr. Rosenberg," said the man. "My name is Aaronson. God is great, he will keep us warm, deliver us from this place, and avenge our plight." The man resumed and even intensified his praying, his body entering a trance.

"At some point tonight, Mr. Aaronson, your eyes will close. You will freeze to death once you fall asleep, Mr. Aaronson. Come sleep with us on the plank."

No response. Father retreated to our designated location for the night.

"Go to sleep now, Sanyi. I'll take the first massage shift."

I folded my frail, emaciated body on top of the small plank, and he started rubbing it. It occurred to me how different my physique became as I managed to fold myself on top of this small, thin rectangle in a fetal position. I fell asleep immediately. He woke me up after what seemed to be minutes, and we exchanged positions.

"I will keep your body warm tonight, don't worry. I will protect you, just like I promised Mother. We will be okay," he didn't hear me because he was already asleep and lightly snoring. His puppy-like snore sounds made me laugh. I started rubbing his cold toes and moved my arms quickly up and down his body. Only a few minutes into my task, my muscles were already aching, and my hands felt heavy. I kept changing angles, positions, and distances, shifting my body weight, altering between hands, elbows, feet, and shoulders doing this delicate work to sustain my strength. At some point, I started feeling as if my energies were about to be depleted and that I would not be able to continue keeping him warm. It made me start crying and my anxieties ran high. That first hour felt like an eternity. To pass time, I recited the list of spices from our store, from A to Z, imagining I was stocking the tidy wooden drawers. Father was there, encouraging and correcting me every time I missed a name.

It was the longest night. We changed roles three times during that night, each of us getting two sessions of sleep. My last shift was much less stressful, and I felt my heartbeat settling down. I was looking around as my hands were rubbing his body. Seemingly, except for me, only the guards on the surrounding watchtowers were awake, the entire camp and bordering nature world were motionless and muted.

Those guards were about my age, I assumed. How are they passing these long hours on their shifts? Are they writing letters to their parents and girlfriends? Are they napping on duty? I fantasized about their warm coats and blankets. What I would not give for a blanket. Their names were Hans, or Franz, or even Alexander. They came from Munich, Frankfurt and Berlin, and a small village outside of Stuttgart. They collected stamps and cared for puppies and loved apple strudels. And now they were wearing the *Wehrmacht* uniform and pointing long rifles at me. What a cruel world we lived in.

In the morning, when the soldiers started walking into our area, I woke him up and we both took a short stroll to stretch our legs. There were a few dead bodies spread around us, prisoners frozen to death overnight. I saw poor Aaronson, his eyes open and lips bluish, lying down alongside two other deceased Jews.

Almost every morning, but especially following cold nights, bodies were being removed from inside and outside the tent and transferred by prisoners in wheelbarrows to the crematorium in the Main Camp. I was experiencing the most pronounced exhibition of Charles Darwin's theories. The best adapted organisms, physically and mentally, survived the KLB nights, while the others perished. It was truly a "natural selection."

After each evening roundup, we would hold each other's hand and run as fast as we could towards the tent. In most cases, we were able to jam into one of the bunks or secure a space on the floor. On other nights, we were left outside the tent, with hundreds of other people. Some nights were almost too long and too hard to survive, others were rather manageable. The wooden plank saved us each of those nights. We would repeat that massaging action, alternating sleep and rub shifts. None of the following outdoor nights was as horrible as the first one. Guarding the plank and making sure we don't lose it to theft became my main everyday responsibility and focus.

Without noticing, we gradually became apathetic and aloof, like everyone surrounding us.

"I don't think I can continue doing this for much longer." Father lost his footing and knelt on one knee. "I'm so tired. This war seems to never end. I don't really care if I die tonight outside."

"Don't speak that way." I also felt too sickly to continue walking around the Small Camp. I was perpetually hungry and dizzy and couldn't really feel the tips of my frozen toes.

"How long can we survive like this? Winter is only getting worse. We should end this nightmare. The Nazi animals are taking pleasure seeing our suffering, I don't wish to give them reasons to be happy."

"You are wrong. Don't lose faith. I'm sure the Russians are on their way to liberate their numerous prisoners of war here," I said. I had absolutely no idea where the Russians were, if they cared about their captured soldiers, or if they had any intention to liberate KLB, but it felt like the right thing to say.

"Do you think Mother is okay?" I changed the subject.

"I don't know, but I'm sure she is fighting like you and me at this instant to stay alive and carry on, so we can meet again in Bratislava when we make it out of here."

I hugged him with a faint grip.

Smoke kept coming out of the crematorium chimney all day and all night. Although Buchenwald was not an extermination camp per se, malnutrition, the cruel winter season, and murderous guard brutality resulted in countless deaths around us. I was imagining the fire burning in those ovens. It must be so warm in that building.

The next day at the afternoon roundup, an SS officer whom we had not yet seen appeared and started calling out names from a typed list. He ordered the persons whose names were read out to step forward to the left side. The last name that he called was Father's. It was the first time since we were captured that we were not on the same name list.

"Come with me," he instinctively whispered and firmly pulled my hand.

"But I'm not on the list! Don't be mad!" I resisted.

"Come with me now and shut up!" he barked at me in a low voice; his eyes firmly focused on the dirt ground.

I had to make a split-second decision and leaped from my spot.

"But they will shoot me!" I whispered to myself. "Have you completely lost your mind?"

I followed him with my eyes staring down and joined the group of 30-odd men who had gathered on the left side. The guards did not conduct a secondary headcount, so no one questioned my presence with them at that point. We were marched out of the Small Camp and into the Big Camp through the iron gate, all the way to the main administration compound.

We were then ordered to stand in five lines outside one of the offices, with two Kapos guarding us.

The door opened, and an officer came out. "Is there anyone present here today who can prepare document translations from German to Polish and Russian and vice versa? Don't waste our time and bother raising your hand unless you are a master at this craft. You have been duly warned."

Father immediately raised his hand. "I can do it! I can do it! I am an expert! Pick me!" he shouted in a stuttering voice. His feeble cry was barely heard.

He was promptly shown the way into the office, while I remained standing in line outside.

The officer then proceeded to call names from the list, and each man whose name was called, went into the office. The two Kapos went inside as well.

And then there were only three of us left in the Small Square: a doe-eyed SS officer and two scrawny prisoners.

Only one prisoner was supposed to be standing there now, in front of the SS officer.

I was the odd man out.

My mind was rushing to calculate my chances, but I couldn't see a sound way to clear the immediate hurdle in front of me. Within seconds, the officer was about to expose me. My tired brain came up with no creative ideas.

The SS officer was staring silently at his notes for a few minutes. He obviously didn't see my prisoner number on any of the printed lists, and that must have broken his rhythm.

Not long after, he erupted.

"You filthy Jew swine! You should be back in the Small Camp," he abruptly shouted at me and came closer. "What are you doing here? Who told you to join this group? I never called out your name or number this morning!"

He was going to hit me, there was doubt about that. Was he one of the excessively violent soldiers? Will he shoot me?

"I'm sorry, Mr. Officer, sir, please... I must have heard the wrong name being called out. Please forgive me, sir. My hearing is not well." I was groveling, blabbering, rambling, pleading for my life. No way was he buying into my bullshitting.

I felt his first kick hit my rib cage, and all the air was sucked out of my lungs. I fell down to the ground and quickly curled, using hands to protect my head and face, crossing my legs to protect my groin. For what felt to me like 15 minutes, he furiously hovered above me, turning me over, kicking the upper part of my body. All I could do was scream: "Father! Help me! Help me! He is killing me!"

Could he hear me inside the office?

"Shout on! No one can hear your screams, you filthy, stupid, ugly Jew," he shouted, as he continued kicking me. He sounded out of breath himself. "You are going to pay for this."

"Help me! Anyone!"

My bleeding head felt dizzy, my hands no longer held on to my ears. I gave up and embraced my doom.

Then someone kicked the office door wide open and shouted in a low voice.

"What's all that raucous out there?" a man in civilian clothes stepped out and asked loudly. Father was standing right behind him. In this scene, there was no doubt who the boss was.

An impressive, tall man wearing a suede jacket, he held his pipe with a clear sense of self-importance and impatience. "Lieutenant Hermann, would you mind explaining why you are beating my poor worker to death?"

The kicking stopped instantly. I took a long breath, but my body was shaking uncontrollably.

"This pig's name was not called out during the selection. He was not supposed to be here," answered Lieutenant Hermann.

"Yeah, yeah, I know. He mistakenly joined his father, who has been doing a fantastic job for me here the last few hours, translating materials. Leave the poor boy be and send him into my office at once. If he's half as talented as Stefan, it would be a real shame to see him go to waste. Much obliged, Lieutenant Hermann."

I was hearing the words coming out of the man's mouth but couldn't work out what was really happening. I must have been half hallucinating. All I remember was that Father ran out, put his shoulder under my arm, held me up, and helped me walk slowly into the office. He gently placed me on a wooden chair.

"Sir, may I take five minutes to cater to my son's wounds? He is bleeding badly. Would you have a first aid kit available?"

"Of course, Stefan. Take that small room and please check back with me in 15 minutes. My assistant will bring you iodine, bandages, and some water shortly. I'm sorry for this unfortunate misunderstanding."

We sat inside the equipment room, and he cleaned and bandaged my face and arms.

"Are you okay?" He hugged me and held back his tears.

"I'll be fine." With my left hand, I was feeling a beating pulse at the edge of my skull, while my right hand was carefully applying pressure to my abdomen, to make sure nothing critical was torn there. "The bruise on the back of my head is really hurting me, and I'm feeling a burn down my stomach, where he repeatedly kicked me. The other cuts and wounds are really nothing. Who is this man who came out to speak with the SS man?"

"His name is Günter. Based on the documents I have been translating in the last hour, I believe he is the civilian in charge of the Gustloff arms factory in Weimar. He spoke to me after I first came in, and he was impressed by my language and writing skills. He seems like a decent man, I think, but we should be very careful. He came here today to select a new group of workers for transfer to the factory."

"I thought that officer was going to kill me. You came for me just in time."

"My dear child, it's a good thing your lungs are in good shape. You screamed so loudly! I heard the shouting and knew it was you. Lucky for us, Günter listened to my pleas. He may be our ticket to survive this camp and make it out alive. We have to be smart. Please follow my instructions carefully. Your body is still in shock, and you may also suffer from a concussion. Don't say anything unless you are asked a direct question or if you are not absolutely sure of what you are doing."

We returned to the main room where Günter was seated with his assistant, and Father went back to translating the documents. I limped to the side of the room, my concerns growing that my spleen or liver were ruptured.

"Let me take a peek at the boy," said Günter and walked closer to me. "Well, you looked like crap out there, but look much better now after washing up. What is your name?"

It was unusual for an educated German to use obscenities.

"Alexander, sir."

Günter smiled. That was the first warm human facial gesture I had experienced with any of our capturers.

"I have a son back home whose name is Alexander, but everyone calls him Lexa. Therefore, I will call you Lexa. Please go and wait with the other workers, Lexa. Stefan still has some work to do for me before we leave."

I sat at the corner of the office with the other workers who were selected to go to the factory.

When Günter and Father completed their work, the manager stood up, yawned, and stretched. "Back to Gustloff, at once," he alerted the soldiers at the entrance with his hands.

All the prisoners left the office and marched towards the two trucks that were parked in the adjacent lot. We were driven to a small sub-camp outside of Weimar, which hosted the forced laborers who worked in the armament factory, just a short distance away. The entire group was taken to the sleeping barracks, composed of simple, wooden sheds. Each prisoner was assigned with a designated bunk bed. My own bed! Father and I shared a bunk. He took the bottom bed; I slept on the top one. We were greeted by factory veterans, who were mostly prisoners of war from the Red Army, but from other countries as well. That evening, I was introduced to captured soldiers from Russia, France, and Poland, and prisoner police officers from Denmark and the Netherlands, speaking a plethora of languages, but mostly communicating in broken German. There were also workers wearing identification marks of homosexuals and Jehovah's Witnesses.

"I thought I had lost you there today," said Father that night after the lights were turned off. "Promise me to take good care of yourself."

"I will make sure you make it out of this alive."

"Me? I'll be fine. Make sure you don't make any silly mistakes. Always think before you act. The cost of an error here could be death."

"Okay."

For the first time in a while, I had trouble falling asleep. Something felt wrong. As if I was overlooking something or missing an important piece of a puzzle.

"What is this Gustloff factory we are in?"

"Just based on the documents I read today, Gustloff is probably one of the largest military compounds in Germany. They employ many thousands of laborers. They produce everything here, from small firearms and ammunition to cannons and antiaircraft machine guns. I think it's a very dangerous place for us to be in, Sanyi, as the allies will for sure bomb it, sooner or later, until they destroy it. For the first time I'm more scared of the American and British pilots than from the German soldiers. Sleep tight and try not to dream of 500-kilogram bombs. Hopefully our luck hasn't run out yet."

That was the missing piece. Yes, we were now cannon fodder here. If the odds continued to stack against Nazi Germany in the war, the likelihood this military complex would not be bombed to the ground was very close to zero.

That was like being stuck between a rock and a hard place. The Nazis winning could not be good for the world and most definitely not good for our family. Alternatively, the destruction of the Nazi industrial military complex in Weimar may be fantastic news for the world, but we would unfortunately be dead, buried under many tons of rubble following massive carpet bombings. I didn't like our chances that night.

6 THE APPRENTICE

I woke up the next morning for my first day as a factory worker. The entire new group that arrived the previous evening from the Small Camp marched into the Gustloff factory together after having breakfast. The sleeping barracks were located a short walking distance from the heavily guarded factory entrance. The building was built above ground, and I could see a steel structure coming out of the ground in a field behind the main building. That was probably an entrance to a bomb shelter.

We formed a line in the wide and empty foyer. I stared at the well-kept chrysanthemum planters along the wall, which conveyed some sense of normalcy and small-town life. There must have been skillful, dedicated gardeners among either the captors or the captives. Günter entered the foyer a few minutes after we did, accompanied by three soldiers. One of them greeted us and started explaining our new state of affairs.

"Going forward you are to be assigned to work on the Gustloff assembly line for the Mauser 337 assault rifles..."

As I learned that day, the Mauser 337 was the most-used personal weapon by the Wehrmacht. I recognized it immediately as

I'd seen it being pointed at me in Sečovce and Bratislava, and its butt was also used to hit Father when we were captured, not very long ago.

"... You will work in this location in two 12-hour shifts, day and night. You will either be assigned to the day or night shift. You will either be working on your shift or remain at your sleeping quarters and will not be allowed anywhere else..."

The production hangar was vast. I could see hundreds of workers sitting, standing, leaning, or carrying equipment and boxes, hundreds of meters deep into the structure. The ceiling was high, and the acoustics created constant overriding echoes.

"Where are Stefan and Alexander Ružiak in this group? Step forward at once."

I was surprised to hear Günter interjecting loudly. He remembered us.

Father slapped the back of my neck, and we both took a step forward.

"Good morning to both of you. Quickly follow me," Günter started walking in long strides.

We hopped and jogged after him.

"I'm putting you both to work inside the spare parts warehouse," he continued while walking, without looking at our direction.

"Stefan, you will be a shift manager at the warehouse. I will introduce you to one of the other managers who can train you. Lexa, you will work at the warehouse but also be responsible for tidying up and cleaning my office every day." He took me to his office, supplied me with a broom, detergents, wipes, and a mop.

"You will start your day every morning by keeping this place spotless and smelling fresh. When you go back home after the war is over, your mother will send me a thank-you note and flowers, I assure you. She will be proud at how adept at cleaning her son has become."

Go back home after the war? Mother sending you flowers? The words coming out of Günter's mouth sounded like a fairytale. *My home was no more. Is my mother still alive? A thank- you note? If my mother were here, she would kill you with her bare hands, Herr Günter, given the chance.*

"After you finish cleaning every day, you will go back down to the assembly line and deliver parts from the spare part warehouse to the line workers," he concluded.

Günter's office was located at the highest level in the hangar, with wide and tall windows overlooking the entire assembly hall with a 360-degree view. He saw everything and was constantly on the lookout. He would use his landline phone to call the shift manager on the floor every time he didn't like what he saw or had a question. He micromanaged the establishment around the clock.

I gave the cleaning job my absolute best: my muscles, heart, and soul. Scrubbing every centimeter of his office, every morning, I didn't rest until the work was done, my hands executing the cleaning tasks frantically. The space became the cleanest location in Gustloff, and probably in the entire Buchenwald area, if not the entire northeastern Germany. There was not a shred of dust behind the remotest of books on the shelf.

Günter appreciated my efforts and was very kind to me, although rarely allowed himself to engage in small talk. The fact that I spoke perfect German surely helped. He sometimes shared the sandwiches his wife prepared with me and allowed me to take his daily newspapers for Father in the warehouse once he was done reading them.

"Lexa, thank you for doing such devoted work cleaning the office. I knew you wouldn't let me down," he said after about two weeks.

"Of course, sir."

"I actually mean it. True, circumstances are such that you are forced to do the work you are doing, and I sincerely regret that. But you are going above and beyond your duties, and that is not going unnoticed by myself and the factory management."

Well, I thought to myself, it's better to be a recognized and appreciated slave than being, well, just a plain slave. Kind words carry weight, even in a forced labor camp. Do they give end-of-year food bonuses for exceptional cleaners?

"Thank you, sir."

I hesitated and continued. "And if you don't mind me saying, the sandwiches you so kindly occasionally share with me are the only remnant I had in recent months of the good life that were and are no more."

Günter smiled. "I will tell Helga; she will be pleased to hear. I will ask her to make a sandwich especially for you, from time to time. Fear not, the war will eventually end, and you will return to your home, raise a family, and eat proper food. I sincerely hope so."

Let's take it in baby steps. I'll take a sandwich first, Günter, thank you very much. We'll talk about homecoming and raising a family some other time.

What a difference a few weeks make. From capture to the cattle car to freezing nights outdoors in the horrid Small Camp and almost being kicked to death to a comfortable life as a factory prisoner apprentice.

My other job was as the spare parts warehouse delivery boy. I operated a low-base, heavy cart, sort of like a wide metal wheelbarrow with four steel wheels, on which I placed crates of parts and supplied them to workstations along the assembly line. Placing the boxes and pushing the cart required significant strength and effort. Mauser parts weighed a ton, as I quickly learned. It only took a few days for my arm and shoulder muscles to pump through my skin.

My main privilege, beyond the daily access to Günter, his polite compliments, and Helga's occasional sandwiches, was the fact that I was only assigned to day shifts, due to my cleaning chores. All other laborers alternated between 12-hour day and night shifts on a weekly basis. Once the shift was over, armed guards would escort the day workers to the sleeping barracks, where we were confined until our next shift.

Also, I was the only factory laborer who had permission to wander around the facility, in order to perform my duties. No other prisoner was allowed to leave their post without permission and an armed soldier escort. If they had to go to the bathroom, they would raise their hand to alert one of the guards who would accompany them on the way there and back. Moreover, no one had permission to speak to any other prisoner on the assembly line. To further separate the laborers, the SS made sure that all the people employed in adjacent workstations were effectively separated in their sleeping quarters. Nevertheless, it was apparent that, despite all the Germans' efforts, some of the laborers who were there before we arrived knew each other well and had developed close relationships. They would walk together to the showers and lavatory. They would stand together in the food line. During shift changes, the day-shift group would walk in one direction, and the night group would walk in the other direction, at the same time. As the two groups passed each other, there were pre-agreed signals to note that all was well and nothing out of the ordinary had occurred during the shift. Very soon it occurred to me that there was a factory underworld I was not yet privy to. My curiosity grew and I wanted to be invited "inside."

"Father, why do you think it is important for the Germans that people who work closely during the shift don't see each other in the barracks?" I asked him late at night.

"That's a good question. I think they want to make sure none of the prisoners are conspiring against them."

"Conspiring? To do what?"

"To break out, to rebel, to turn on the guards, to sabotage the weapon production process. Anything prisoner soldiers would do, given the opportunity and means."

"But it would be foolish for anyone to rebel. The war is most likely about to end, everyone says that. Why would anyone risk being caught and then executed? What is there for them to gain?"

"Well, Sanyi, we don't know for a fact that the war is nearing its end. And people are angry and proud and want to take their revenge on their enemies. These prisoners are soldiers and policemen, they are trained to fight and revolt."

"We should absolutely not participate in any such activity. We shouldn't betray Günter's confidence and trust after all he's done for us. Good night."

Scientists termed the Stockholm Syndrome, a condition in which hostages develop an emotional bond with their captors during captivity. During these first weeks, I would have probably been a prime candidate for a Stockholm Syndrome research work. Günter was the first person who treated me like a human being during our long years of surreal existence, first as hiding refugees and now as lowlife prisoners. At the same time, Günter was a true, proud German, embodying a nation that enslaved and murdered our family and people. I was mature enough to understand that not all Germans were Nazis, not all Nazi collaborators were essentially bad people, and not everyone was brave enough to oppose the cruel and dangerous wave of fascism that was drowning Europe. Was Günter a Nazi who got his will by being a nice guy or was Günter a nice, albeit not brave, guy who was doing his best to manage the Nazi "situation" he was forced into dealing with? At night on the bunk bed, I hoped that he was the latter. I convinced myself that there were millions of people like him. Or, more accurately, I wanted to be sure that there were millions of people like him. That had to be the case. Otherwise, what was the point in fighting and saving a world with so many bad people in it? And if so, was there a path to fighting and beating the Germans while protecting all the Günters who were surrounding us? How could I be sure that Günter was, at his core, a good person? I knew it wasn't possible.

I became highly skilled at my trade, knew exactly where to position myself across the assembly line, how to collect packages in the warehouse, and how to hand over the parts along the various stations to other prisoners. As I was the only person allowed to speak with the men on the floor, I got to know many of them. The guards were standing far away from most stations, allowing me numerous chances to exchange a few words with laborers.

These discussions taught me a lot about the weapons we were producing. When the Mauser was marked with the letters "bcd" or the number "337," it meant that the rifle was assembled at Gustloff. Both "bcd" and "337" were similar models derived from the Mauser 98K prototype. The various parts were manufactured in multiple facilities around Germany, shipped to Gustloff, and were assembled here. The Mauser 337 was originally a Czech design, and the technology was brought from Czechoslovakia to Germany during the 1930s.

One early afternoon during our second week at Gustloff, I was running my usual rounds across the assembly line. When I halted the cart at my first station to hand out the bolts, the prisoner at the station stared at me and started speaking in Russian.

"My name is Grischa." He pointed at himself. "What is your name?"

"I am Lexa," I answered. I understood him because Slovak and Russian are quite similar.

Grischa was a majestic specimen of a Russian army officer. He was about 35. His build, posture, direct talk, and articulated sentences implied leadership, authority, and strength. He was likely a high-ranking Red Army commander. He had a bright, blond, European facade, unlike many of the Russians workers in the factory, who had darker skin and eyes.

"Come closer to me, Lexa, I want to speak quietly." He gestured with his fingers.

I took a step closer and turned around so as not to face Grischa and arouse any guard's suspicion and fiddled with the metal widgets on my cart.

"Listen Lexa, you are walking around the building, visiting every corner, every day. I want you to do something for me."

I felt cold chills but didn't reply. For days I'd been waiting to be contacted by the "underground powers" in the factory but could never imagine how those powers would present themselves to me. The moment had arrived.

"There is a Russian named Yosipov at the end of the assembly line." He pointed discreetly. "He is the person whose job is to heat up the barrels with the flame to solder the rifle sight using tin. Tell Yosipov that Grischa said that he should cut in half the amount of tin he puts under the upper sight when connecting it to the barrel." His hands marked what a normal dose of matter looked like, and what "half" would be.

This was a rather long and complicated sentence in Russian for me to decipher, so I shook my head to signal that I didn't fully understand. He kept on saying *Zin* [tin] and, at some point, I figured it out, and moved on with my cart.

I had a couple of hours to consider my next move. Do I play it safe, refuse to collaborate, and risk the wrath of a factory underground movement, or indeed become a soldier in the makeshift army set out to crush the Nazis, with all the risks involved? That same question was repeatedly going through my mind at night. Now this was no longer a theoretical exercise. It was time to decide. There was no opportunity to obtain Father's blessing, nor was there time for internal debate. Actually, I was relieved to know that the answer was intuitively, crystal clear in my mind.

At the end of my round, I reached Yosipov, whose station was the last in the assembly line. I was already quite familiar with the process he was responsible for.

Yosipov's job was to weld the upper sight of the rifle. He would firmly place the barrel and the bolt into forceps that only allowed the barrel to rotate. Below his station was a furnace that generated a powerful orangey flame that was heating the exact area on the barrel where the sight was to be welded. Yosipov would hold a thin tin rod where the flame made contact with the rotating barrel, and after the tin melted, he would firmly install the sight chassis using tongs to validate the accuracy of the sight location. The upper sight had a smaller, more delicate sight that could be adjusted to the right or to the left. As my eyes again studied the process that Yosipov performed, it was clear that if significantly less tin was to be used in the soldering process, the sight chassis would become loose once the barrel absorbed any type of a strong blow during battle. When that happened, the Mauser would be deemed utterly useless, because the shooter wouldn't be able to accurately aim. I understood the genius behind Grischa's plan, obviously a result of years of army field experience. The Mauser would never absorb such a meaningful hit while in the factory, so the act of sabotage would not immediately be traced back to the assembly line. The impact on the rifle, and hence damage to the sight, would only be absorbed much later, during actual battle.

"Yosipov, my name is Lexa. You have a message from Grischa." I used my hands theatrically as I spoke quietly in Slovak, instinctively pointing to the location of Grischa's station.

Yosipov didn't even turn his head. I knew he was fully focused and attentive because he put down his tools when he heard the name Grischa.

"He asks that you cut the amount of tin you melt into each barrel by half." I used the same sign language used by Grischa to show what "half" looked like.

He turned his head to look at me and nodded. His eyes told me the message was clearly received and understood.

That week, Father was working night shifts, so we didn't see each other almost at all. After dinner, I went into the lavatory. Together with me entered Thomas, a Danish policeman whose bunk was close to ours. We had never spoken a word between us, but he was one of the men who introduced themselves to us on our first day. I also saw him working in the assembly line.

"Your name is Lexa, right?" he asked in German.

I nodded.

"Be very careful, Lexa. There are eyes and ears everywhere, watching all of us, constantly." He left the room before I had a chance to turn my head towards him.

I went back to my bunk, and my heart was pounding. What did Thomas know? Was he an informer or a friendly? Was I careless in my actions? What part of my actions could have exposed me? What would happen to me if I got caught? I had promised Mother to take care of Father. I couldn't do foolish things like helping the POWs in their sabotage schemes. Also, Günter saved our lives and built confidence in Father and me. It would be foolish to betray that confidence.

I didn't sleep one minute that night.

The next day, I was determined to do my work professionally and not engage in risky shenanigans with my coconspirators. I was so confused. I wanted to help Grischa and Yosipov and their collaborators, because they were fighting the good fight, our fight. But at the same time, I couldn't risk my life, because I knew he would never survive without me. I desperately needed his advice.

I avoided Grischa as much as I could.

Two days later, Father went back to day shifts.

That night, I whispered in his ear. "I need your advice. I started helping some of the workers who are attempting to sabotage the weapons."

His eyes widened.

I decided not to tell him about my encounter with Thomas, or to disclose the names or identities of Grischa or Yosipov. "I've been very careful. They are Russians. I think they are smart and know what they are doing. I want to help them defeat the Nazis, but I need your blessing. I won't do this anymore unless you tell me that it's okay, because it is putting us both at risk."

He hugged me and kissed my cheek. He very rarely kissed me. "I'm proud of you, Sanyi. Do it. Do it and don't be scared. I don't know if we'll live to tell this story, but we owe it to your mother and our dead family members to fight these bastards."

I expected him to say exactly that, and still couldn't go on participating in these activities without hearing the words coming out of his pale lips. He was so weak, so far removed from his homeland and comfortable bourgeois life.

"I will make you proud. I will bring us both back to see Mother."

That night, and for the first time, I had a dream about orchestrating a mass sabotage operation. In my dream, I was walking along a paved road while lines of German tanks, armored vehicles, and horse-drawn cannons were passing me by. As they were driving next to me, I reached out and, using my bare hands, bent the cannon barrels, dismantled armored tank chains, pulled apart flamethrowers, and knocked down jeeps. This dream kept recurring in various versions.

Walking about the assembly line, I started thinking of my own ways of meddling with the Mauser. A few days later, when I visited Grischa, he pointed at a box of cartridge extractor pins I had on my cart.

"The next time you stop in Yosipov's station, grab these little pieces of steel, and when the guards are not looking, heat them for only a few seconds in the flame coming out of the furnace. Do you understand?"

I nodded my head up and down. The previous day, I had the exact same thought. I didn't even need Grischa to complete his sentence.

The cartridge extractor pin was a small, steel, tooth-like widget, extremely robust, that was installed inside the bolt. After the rifle operator fired the Mauser, the bolt would open, this "tooth" would go into the cartridge, and discard it. The "tooth" was so robust that it was extremely difficult to fit it into the bolt during the assembly process. Keeping it for a few seconds inside Yosipov's flame, the steel would soften, and forever lose its robustness. After shooting several rounds, as many as ten perhaps, the softened tooth would snap, deeming the Mauser utterly unusable. Grischa's genius struck me again. The Germans would never find out about this on the assembly floor, or even after shooting one or two rounds at a range. The impact would only take place on the battlefield, at the worst possible time for the rifle's owner.

Every other day, I started heating up these steel teeth using Yosipov's furnace. I planned and perfected a position where it was not possible for any guard to see what my hand was doing when it was nearing the furnace.

During the time we spent together, Grischa taught me all there was to know about firearms. He had the rare skill and ability to break down his tutoring into short, daily tutorials that connected in my mind and gave me a plethora of creative, destructive ideas. I learned from him that during a long recoil action, such as the one used by the Mauser 337, the barrel and bolt recoil all the way back as an integral unit. Once its rearward movement is absorbed by its recoil spring, the barrel is forced forward by the spring, where it unlocks from the bolt and returns to battery. The bolt, after compressing its own recoil spring, is held in the rearmost position until the barrel returns to battery. At this point, the fired shell has been extracted and ejected, and a new shell has been lifted from the magazine. The bolt is released by the return of the barrel and is forced-closed by its recoil spring.

"Are you ready for our next project?" asked Grischa and he smiled.

"I am, Commander Grischa."

He was now looking to meddle with the rifle's stock. "Listen, this one will be more difficult to execute because of a language barrier. The guy who is working on the stocks is a Frenchman, and so far, I have not been able to communicate with him. You will have to figure out how to bridge the language gap."

Christophe, the French prisoner, used air-pressure screwdrivers to tighten the bolt to the wooden stocks using long, firm screws. The grooves into which the screws were inserted were received in the factory after having already been carved in the wood. Christophe's station had a large round air pressure meter, like the ones you would see in gas stations.

"Find a way to direct Christophe to increase the air-pressure in the pump from 300 to 400 atmospheres when inserting the screws," Grischa instructed. He explained that this would apply excessive pressure on the turning screws, resulting in the widening of the grooves. The higher the air pressure applied, the looser the screw would become inside the groove. Only a few bumps and hits on the wooden stock, and the Mauser would lose its stability.

While I spoke German, Hungarian, Czech, Slovak, Yiddish, some English, and by now some Russian, unfortunately French was not spoken in our milieu. When I arrived at Christophe's station, I tried whispering in each of the languages, only to see him shaking his head, time and again.

I had to use my pantomime skills to introduce Grischa's newest scheme, using my fingers to symbolize "300" and "400." Christophe looked at me eventually and released a cunning smile. He lifted his right hand towards the round air-pump regulator, and slowly turned it to the right, until it reached 400 atmospheres. I smiled and left.

I reported back to Grischa the next day.

"Good job, Lexa. We are a good team."

We looked at each other. In what parallel universe would a soon-to-be 17-year-old, spoiled only child, Jewish boy from rural Eastern Slovakia and a high-ranking communist military officer become partners in crime? Only in Buchenwald.

"When you did your last round, I saw you with Christophe and the atmospheric meter and it hit me. I have found the ultimate sabotage project." He smiled.

I already thought Grischa was the smartest person I had ever met. What did he have in store for the Germans now?

"The process of assembling the barrel and the bolt is extremely critical. We are now going to interfere with it," he adamantly stated. "Come back tomorrow and I will share my plan."

That evening I saw Thomas walking in the barracks, but he turned his eyes away. I was looking for any signal but couldn't identify one.

In the morning, Grischa walked me through his new plan. I was rather comfortable spending time in his station, slowly offloading packages, and that allowed us time to communicate in detail. My Russian improved markedly during the time we'd been communicating.

He explained that the bare barrel, with a conic worn on its edge, was held by a humongous lathe. The bolt was gripped by the lathe on the other side and was rotated at high speeds. Both pieces were on opposite sides of a canal, with an engine advancing the bolt towards the barrel for the screwing. The process of screwing the barrel to the bolt was regulated by an air pressure meter, like the one used by Christophe in his process. Applying extreme rotating pressure would result in the disintegration of the bolt. The idea was to only increase the pressure slightly, in order to crack the bolt, without breaking it. Under higher pressures, the metal reaches a point where it can no longer rotate, and the energy applied by the rotating motor causes the cracks to occur. A Mauser with severe cracks in its bolt would have limited shooting distance capability, due to energy loss through the cracks; a soldier aiming at a target 800 yards away, would be disappointed to see his bullet land after only 400 yards, because of weaker propulsion.

"The person handling the pressure gauge is Vladimir." He pointed at him for me. "Go ask Vladimir to raise the pressure from 150 to 180."

Unlike our previous schemes, this one felt more dangerous to me.

"Won't they find out about this rather easily when testing the Mauser in a shooting range?" I asked.

"I thought about that too. If my assumptions are correct, they would only test it for short target practice, roughly about 100 yards. They will see nothing," assured Grischa.

By now, I fully trusted his judgment.

Vladimir, another Russian POW, was much easier to communicate with than Christophe, the French prisoner. Once I mentioned Grischa's name, Vladimir straightened up and devoted his full attention to my instructions. After listening, he nodded, turned to me, and winked.

"Don't worry, it will be done," he said in Russian.

Weeks went by. I continued practicing and improving my Russian with the help of Grischa, and also chatted with Yosipov and Vladimir. I became fluent quickly.

The upper sights, cartridge extractors, wooden stocks, barrels, and bolts were now partly assembled in accordance with Grischa's specifications, depending on the shift compilations, seemingly unnoticed.

One evening on the bunk bed, I tried to statistically quantify the ratio of rifles produced in our assembly line that had at least one faulty process in their production. My estimate was that those represented the lion's share of the factory's output. The idea of hundreds of German soldiers storming American infantry or a Russian post only to have their rifles fail at the moment of truth was purely blissful.

Factory life was hard, monotonous but by all means so much better than our time at the Small Camp in Buchenwald. We began focusing on the mundane life aspects of the prisoner-worker universe. It was easy to forget that we were at a Nazi weaponry factory adjacent to a concentration camp in a constantly bombarded battle area where the Red Army and Allied armored divisions were battling SS and Wehrmacht forces.

Every prisoner had a weekly allowance of two cigarettes, courtesy of factory management. Neither of us smoked, so we stockpiled our allocations for bartering purposes, and managed to accumulate a respectable stash of smokes. Eventually, I helped him trade our entire cigarette pile in exchange for a thick, dark winter coat, with fancy white buttons. Unlike me, Father was suffering gravely from the cold. The coat made his days and nights, when most of his shifts were scheduled, much more bearable.

With time, I became friendly with a Czech prisoner named Zdeněk, originally from Prague, who was almost always staffed in day shifts, and whose bunk was close to ours. He wasn't Jewish. He didn't tell me why he was imprisoned, and I didn't ask. He didn't ask me either. We found it entertaining to communicate about everything but the big, painful things. We spoke about the accumulating snow, tasteless soup, the rats swarming the barracks corridors, and our plans for after the war. Zdeněk, who was studying at a university before the war, wanted to become a math teacher. I told him I wanted to become a locksmith and have my own retail shop in Bratislava.

One morning during the shift change, I was marching within the day shift line towards the factory, and we were adjacent to the night shift group that had just left the factory and walked the other direction. Suddenly, Father, who was ending his shift, broke away from his line and approached me. He walked alongside me for a few seconds, weeping, hugged me with both hands and gave me a kiss. His body was sweaty and shivering, and I was totally dumbfounded.

"Be strong, Sanyi, my dear boy," he said with tears in his eyes. "We shall not be seeing each other again. I didn't do it! I love you, take care of Mother."

This only took a few seconds, after which he disengaged and ran back to join his group, walking towards the sleeping barracks.

I was in complete shock. What would make him do and say such a thing? What "didn't he do"? Did he lose his mind? Which one of us was in grave danger of death? Were the Germans on to my underground activities? What could I do to find out? I had only one trustworthy and knowledgeable person to turn to.

Entering the assembly hall, instead of climbing to my employer's office, I took the cart all the way down to Grischa's station to learn if he knew anything.

"Grischa, is my father in danger?" I asked, trying to hide my bursting emotions. "He manages the spare part warehouse."

"Hmm. Rumor is that two prisoners managed to break out of the factory during the night shift. Do you know anything about that?"

My wide-open eyes signaled that I didn't.

"Okay. The guards found a broken window in the spare parts warehouse and concluded that the prisoners used insider help to get inside the warehouse and break out through the window. They couldn't find any evidence of breaking into the warehouse by use of force. If your father oversaw the warehouse during the night shift, he is in a very difficult situation now. I'm sorry, Lexa."

My mouth dried up. He would never do that without consulting me. Or would he? Maybe he wanted to also participate in our efforts? Why didn't he tell me about it?

It was time to move to the next station before drawing unnecessary attention. I thanked Grischa and pressed ahead. The thoughts came from all directions. If what Grischa said was true, he was doomed. Could this be true? Would he risk himself in this manner without letting me know? Did he help them escape and get caught? This didn't really sound like him. He just wouldn't do this. What was the right move now? By the time my round was finished, I was able to think straight again. Regardless of whether or not he collaborated with the escapees, there was only one thing I could do for him.

I went up to clean Günter's office.

"Good morning, Lexa," he said.

"Good morning, sir."

I burst into tears, told him what Father had done during the shift change and added the rumors I had heard, obviously without mentioning Grischa, and said there was no way that he could be responsible. Günter confirmed the rumors to be true.

"I regret to inform you, Lexa, that I have been notified by the SS commander this morning that Stefan is suspected of being complicit in this criminal act, and that he is to be sentenced to death by a firing squad tomorrow by the same SS commander. It was most disheartening for me to hear, after all that I have done for both of you. I respected Stefan. Didn't think he would act so foolishly."

"You must believe me, sir, Father would never do such a thing. He is a man of honor and discipline. He would never betray your trust." I was on my knees in front of him. "More so, he is a family man. He would never put his only son at such risk. Please, you must believe me!"

Günter paused and tilted his chair back. He deliberated with himself.

"Your arguments make sense to me, knowing Stefan. I must say that it was difficult for me to believe the terrible news when I first heard them. Stefan is a true professional and has earned my respect, and I owe it to him to at least further investigate other explanations regarding this prisoner escape."

I held my breath and stared at him. For Father and me, Günter was now playing God, judge, and jury, for the second time.

"Come with me," Günter barked at me. He climbed down the stairs hastily, and I walked closely after him.

We circled the perimeter of the spare parts warehouse, through the inner part of the assembly hall. The two spaces were separated by a wall. The lower part of the wall was made of thick wooden planks, with desks attached to them. The upper part was made of thick, unbreakable glass.

Günter was examining the area thoroughly and sharing his thoughts aloud. "The only possible way to enter the warehouse unnoticed from the assembly hall is to go through one of the wooden planks, below a desk," he concluded, detective-style.

We circled the entire floor, with Günter bending under each and every desk and checking whether all the planks were intact and properly connected to the structural beams. All of a sudden, in one of the corners of the hall, he identified a loose plank. As soon as Günter touched it, the plank fell into the inner space of the warehouse, making a loud noise.

Günter paused.

"Lexa, you just saved Stefan's life." He got back on his feet, a proud grin on his face. "These escaped prisoners entered the warehouse by loosening and moving this wooden plank. Kindly go up and wait for me in my office."

Günter wasted no time and went to speak with the SS officer to update him of his investigative work and findings, carrying the missing plank with him. Father's name was cleared that same morning.

When Günter came back to the office, I asked him to arrange for me to be accompanied by a guard to go back to the barracks and update Father, who was otherwise going nuts expecting a firing squad to be coming for him. I also feared he would harm himself.

"You are a good son, Lexa. I will arrange for you to take the rest of the shift off to go and spend time with Stefan. On behalf of the factory management, please accept my sincerest apologies and share them also with Stefan."

I still couldn't figure out my feelings towards Günter. Undoubtedly, he was playing the field for Satan's team, but I now knew for a fact that there were angels down in hell.

The Rosenbergs got to live another day.

7 AIR RAID

Throughout our time as factory laborers, the air raid sirens went off day in and day out. Father and I were horrified to hear them the first time, but our bunk partners explained it was a usual routine. However, our factory had not been bombed even once during the first months of our stay there.

These loud alarm noises became part of the perpetual factory soundtrack, combined with machine and background clamor. They'd become white noise. I pictured the British and American pilots flying high overhead. Did they know about us, prisoners of war, homosexuals, Jews, Gypsies, and the rest of the captives who were held as live targets on German soil? It seemed reasonable to think that our lives were considered expendable, acceptable sacrifices in the global efforts to topple Hitler and the Third Reich. You stupid leaders, generals, pilots, you should have bombed the extermination camps, the concentration camps, the crematoriums, the administration offices where clerks spent months compiling killing lists of Jews and Gypsies while sipping tea and smoking cigarettes, years ago. These were all big, fat targets on the maps of Europe. Not easily missed. It's not too late!

No bombs were dropped on us just yet, but we did hear distant, faint explosions that could only be the result of air raids. According to Grischa, the Zeiss factories in Jena, only 30 kilometers away, had already been bombed a number of times in 1944.

Everything changed the morning of February 9, 1945.

It was one of the coldest days of the year. The ground was covered with thick layers of ice and fresh snow as we were marching, making our way to start the day shift. The sky was clear and blue. Just before entering the building, the sky became gray with metal objects. We saw high flying planes appearing right above us. There were many dozens of them, if not hundreds. The alarm started blasting a few minutes earlier, but we didn't make much of it. We heard that alarm go off almost every day.

According to the air raid procedure, our guards would stay in their positions to make sure we didn't escape or use this opportunity to arm ourselves, while the rest of the German staff, civilian and SS, hurried into the bunker.

Then we heard the whistle of first bombs. A dropped bomb generates a unique, high-pitched sound.

After the whistles came formidable explosions all around us. Mass panic ensued.

Immediately, the air-raid procedure was scrapped; the guards left their posts and ran for their lives, through the factory door, into the bunker, shouting frantically in German for us to steer clear of their way.

Now unguarded, horrified by the unbearable whistle and explosion sounds, the prisoners left their posts and started running feverishly after the guards towards the bunker. I obviously joined them. The entrance door to the bunker was open, and a large group of prisoners, including me, managed to enter. One of the workers running next to me was Zdeněk. I didn't know where Father was. He worked the night shift the previous day and was probably sleeping in the barracks when the planes arrived. I couldn't run to get him, and hoped he was awake and making his way to the bunker.

Located under the paved road leading to the factory, the bunker was made from solid concrete. To enter the bunker, you had to go through an elevated sand hill in the factory yard, leading from the road. The bunker was a massive, submarine-like divided space, with multiple sealed chambers. Each chamber had a steel door, with a large, round metal lock that had to be rotated to open.

Inside the bunker was utter chaos. Soldiers, ununiformed personnel, and prisoners were shouting and running in all directions. Zdeněk and I found ourselves as part of a group of about 50 people, including SS, German civilians, and a few prisoners, in one of the chambers. Two of the SS soldiers sealed the room from the inside. It was obvious that if the bunker absorbed a direct bomb hit, all would share the same grisly fate. The exposed concrete would not be able to absorb the impact of a 500-kilogram bomb. Without coordination, we were all looking up, staring at the ceiling, as if our minds were able to jointly hypnotize and maneuver the bombs away from their path.

The bomb whistles were getting closer and closer, and the noise of the explosion impact was getting louder and louder. Dozens of explosions were clearly heard for over an hour.

We then heard a loud, sharp whistle, and life went into slow motion.

After the whistle came a colossal boom.

My eyes closed and I felt great pressure tossing me towards the wall. I instinctively put my head between my legs, under my arms. My ears were ringing, and I felt nauseous. After a few moments that felt like a lifetime, it became very cold. I slowly opened my eyes and saw the blue sky above me. The bunker ceiling was no longer there. It had been blown to pieces, dust and debris were everywhere. The sky was clear, not a cloud in sight, and the planes were no longer flying above. One could only see the thick smoke coming up from the massive building that earlier that morning used to be the Gustloff armament factory.

There was a silence accompanied by a loud background buzzing sound. Those were probably my ears ringing.

First, I counted the fingers in both my hands. Then, using my fingers, I slowly started feeling my entire body, moving systemically from head to toe, making sure nothing was missing or mutilated. It was all there.

Zdeněk was sitting next to me, his eyes wide open. He then blinked. He was alive, and at first glance looked to be in one piece as well.

I looked around the large, shattered chamber. Body parts and blood were all around the ruins of the bunker. My ears were still ringing loudly, but inside that ring I started hearing gut-wrenching cries for help from the wounded.

Tears started rolling down my face. People who stood next to me a few minutes before, Germans and prisoners, were lying around, in pieces, squashed by large chunks of concrete and torn by bomb shrapnel.

"Let's get away from here, the planes might come back any minute to finish us off," I told Zdeněk. I couldn't hear myself speak and was probably shouting.

He was pale as a ghost and just nodded his head up and down.

He followed me as I crawled through the rubble and piles of human bodies, mutilated, and rendered unrecognizable by blood and dirt. We slipped out through a wide hole in the external concrete wall, to the icy factory yard.

The moment we were out, the first planes from the second wave were arriving above us, and the air raid resumed. Bombs were whistling around again. Zdeněk and I ran as far away from the shattered factory as our feet could carry us, toward the farmhouses of a nearby, small village. We stopped to catch our breath next to a big, old hay barn. An old German woman was standing on her front porch, in the adjacent wooden house. She saw that we were running away from the factory and tracked our progress.

"Wait a minute, wait a minute, my children!" she shouted in our direction. "I have some food for you!"

We cautiously stopped and drew near. She walked towards us,

holding freshly baked pumpernickel bread and a jar of pickles. The smell of warm bread blended with that of gunpowder and burnt flesh.

As I came close and reached out my hand to take the food, she could easily spot my prisoner number stitched on top of the yellow triangle.

"May God bless and save you, my children," she said, making the sign of the cross and went back into her house.

We kept on running as the explosion noises faded away. All was suddenly quiet. We were about seven kilometers away by now. I couldn't stop thinking about Father and had a terrible feeling that he hadn't escaped and was badly hurt or dead.

"What do we do now?" asked Zdeněk. "I think we should keep on running. Let's find a place to hide. We can then think what direction is safest to advance."

"I can't come with you, Zdeněk. My father is back there in the factory, and I have to return and see if he needs my help." There was no hesitation in my voice, not a doubt in my mind. "But honestly, I am not sure we can successfully escape in this freezing cold, surrounded by armed German forces everywhere. I think you should come back with me."

After deliberating for a few minutes, Zdeněk agreed to return with me.

We waited for 30 more minutes to make sure the planes were not coming back. Then, we started making our way back to the factory compound. On the way, Zdeněk met a few of his Czech comrades, and I continued alone.

Huge bomb craters were everywhere.

I walked slowly, my feet plunging through a mix of snow and mud. Because my thoughts were so preoccupied with Father, I didn't notice that one of my shoes had gotten lost in the deep snow. I turned around to trace back my steps but couldn't find it. I finally made it back to the compound. All the wooden sheds used for sleeping were destroyed. While those buildings were not directly impacted by the bombs, their fragile structures couldn't withstand the overwhelming bombing, and were now piles of rubble. I identified the pile that used to be our sleeping shed and tried to move pieces of wood that used to be the ceiling, to clear my path. I crawled in and reached our bunk bed. He used to sleep in the lower bunk. He was not there.

Hours had passed since the fateful morning bombing. Around me, in the wreckage, were dead bodies and debris. I was now shouting, crying loudly for him using both his original and assumed names, stepping on human remains on my way out. Outside the ruined shed, I saw a group of French prisoners and immediately recognized Christophe. As soon as he spotted me, he called my name.

"Lexa... Papa!" He used his hands and voice intonation to signal that they had taken him to one of the last standing sheds, which he pointed me to.

I started running as fast as I could on my single shoe. There were still a few sheds standing intact around the perimeter. Apparently, the prisoners emptied all the beds and equipment from one of them, to make room for the dead and wounded. I stepped into the shed and passed through the long line of bodies and badly injured men. I inspected all of them twice. Poor Yosipov was lying there, dead, his face colorless, eyes open. I tried to erase that picture from my mind and turned away to look for Father.

I could not recognize his face in any of the men lying there. It didn't make sense. Christophe had told me that he had been brought there. Walking out in desperation, I held my head and couldn't figure it out. And then it occurred to me.

The coat. The white buttons. No one in the factory had a coat like his. When surveying the men inside, I only looked at their faces, but not at their clothes.

I reversed my path and ran back in, examining the line of men on the floor, until I managed to spot the white buttons. I knew it was him, but his face was unrecognizable. It was swollen and filled with small, bloody slashes. I started checking him more closely. He had the same cuts all over his exposed body parts. I opened his thick coat and placed my ear on his chest. He was breathing, yet unconscious. His heart was beating. I had no idea what my next move was, but I knew that whatever it was, I needed a pair of shoes first.

Instinctively, I first went out and brought fresh snow, to wash off the blood and dirt from his face, hands, and feet. I took off pieces of clothing from dead prisoners lying next to him. Some pieces I used to cover him and increase his body temperature; others I used to warm myself. I also managed to find a pair of shoes my size to replace my single remaining one. The poor man I took them from wouldn't be needing them anymore. He had to be moved for medical attention, so I went outside to seek help.

Near the shed stood a Russian prisoner who was a medical assistant in the factory. I ran and grabbed him.

"My father, he is dying. You have to help him, quickly. Please."

He came with me and examined the patient briefly. "He will make it," he said. "I do not know why he is unconscious, but he will be fine."

I massaged his hands and feet, like we used to do to each other during the cold nights in Buchenwald's Small Camp, trying to wake him up.

He wouldn't wake up.

People started shouting outside.

"The Red Cross trucks from the Buchenwald infirmary are here! They are parked on the main road!"

The shed that hosted the wounded was located on the opposite side of the main road. That would be a long walk, carrying a wounded person in the snow.

I quickly lifted a dislocated door from the ground and ran out with it, looking for the group of French prisoners I saw earlier. They were enjoying a smoke a few hundred yards away.

"Papa!" I shouted, lifting the door, trying to use my hands to demonstrate the action of carrying a stretcher.

They figured it out immediately and rushed towards me, helping to load Father on top of the door, and three of them joined me in carrying him outside, in quick steps through the heavy snow and mud, in the direction of the makeshift Red Cross station.

As we were walking through the mud, Father's body was bouncing up and down and moving around side to side, absorbing all sorts of hits. His eyes suddenly opened. Surprisingly, he was in a rather good mood.

"Are you okay, Father? Are you in pain?" I yelled.

"I think I'm okay. But my shoulder is killing me," he answered, trying to hold on to the door with one hand.

We got to the Red Cross truck and loaded the door, with Father on it, onto the giant, open trunk. When I tried to climb up and join him, one of the German soldiers pushed me back down.

"No place here for the healthy and well. Get lost!"

The truck was stocked up with wounded prisoners and then took off to Buchenwald later that afternoon.

I was left alone, not knowing if I'd ever see Father again. I looked around me. The factory was gone. All that was left was a huge pile of rubble. The guards were gone. Dozens of bodies were piled on the ground. There was no food, no supplies, nowhere to escape the cold as the sleeping barracks were flattened. I couldn't see any of the people who worked with me in the factory other than Christophe. It then occurred to me that I hadn't seen Günter after the raid, and that saddened me. I assumed the worst for him.

"Hey, Lexa! Come with us. We are going to pick some food," Christophe shouted at me and used his hand gestures to symbolize a meal.

I joined the French prisoners, as they walked towards the snow-covered village fields. We walked around for a while, and I didn't understand what they were looking for. What were they looking to pick in the middle of winter? They repeatedly leaned down and dug holes in the snow, exposing green layers of leaves.

"Look here, Lexa," said Alain, one of the French prisoners who spoke reasonable German.

I knelt next to him on the cold ground.

"These leaves are good for you. They are *Stellaria Media*, or winter weeds," he said as he pointed to small greens which I remembered as a child from the fields back in Sečovce. "They have very good nutritional value."

I pulled a handful of leaves and stuffed them into my mouth. It was the best salad I had ever had.

"Come over there with me," he told me and started walking.

Before catching up with him, I made sure to hoard two pockets full of winter weeds.

"Now look at these. They are called *Nasturtium*, it's a type of watercress that is common in these areas," he pointed at thick stalks with larger green leaves he exposed in the snow. "They are very good for you, packed with vitamins."

This one tasted even better than the first plant. I emptied my pockets of the winter weeds, filled my mouth with as many as I could, and refilled the pockets with my new favorite green.

"Stand up, I want to show you one more thing," said Alain, who walked faster than any other person I've seen, while not being threatened by a German Mauser.

He cleared the snow from a spot about 20 yards away.

"Whatever you do, however hungry you become, never eat this. You will die very quickly," he said with an animated motion of his hand slitting his throat. "This plant is from the Aconitum family."

Honestly, these leaves all looked the same to me. I thanked Alain and started thinking of a survival game plan. Using rock placement, I made sure to mark the areas where they picked the watercress and winter weeds. I didn't want to die consuming the cursed Aconitum.

Over the following few hours, the French taught me more valuable survival tips, and I stuffed my belly full of leaves. I became, at least temporarily, a member of the French crew. We took large pieces of broken wooden walls from the destroyed sheds and used them to block a small area where we could find refuge from the wind and snow, so we could sleep. We kept warm during the night with extra blankets and coats that we stripped from dead bodies. During the day, we hunted for food. Otherwise, I wandered around, curious, examining the wreckage, and keeping to myself. We hardly had any supervision. The chaos of war and devastation was all around us. The smell of burnt flesh, simmered by freezing temperatures and smoke.

Another day went by. German teams came and went, attempting to restore some order. There were no longer armed guards in sight, but not one of prisoners around me tried to escape. We were mentally fatigued, malnourished, and had nowhere to go in the freezing temperatures of the German winter. I didn't want to give any German an excuse to shoot at me. Finding Father was the only priority on my mind.

On the third day in the wrecked factory ground, while passing alongside an administration building at the corner of the compound, a German officer came out of the door and shouted at me.

"Jew! Come over here this instant."

There was no choice, I had to follow his orders and was beating myself over getting into this situation. My problem had always been that I could never sit still, my curiosity had me always walking around. I practically went looking for trouble, and that's why I kept finding it.

I went over to the officer and followed him. He led me into one of the adjacent buildings that was apparently turned into an ad hoc kitchen following the bombardment. We entered a huge refrigerator room. The officer took out a gigantic keg of fresh milk and poured me a healthy cup. He must have seen me walking outside with my piteous, slender appearance, and his conscience made him offer me some dairy.

"Drink!" he ordered.

Of all the putrid survivors, the German had to pick the one who was lactose intolerant. I could not digest milk in an era when no one knew what lactose was and whether people developed intolerance to it. Moreover, I had not had anything to eat but cow grass and thin leaves for three days. My stomach would never be able to withstand this unwanted ingredient.

"I'm sorry, but I can't," I murmured.

"What's the matter with you, Jew?" exclaimed the astonished officer.

"I'm terribly sorry, Mr. Officer. Thank you for your extraordinary generosity, but I just can't drink milk. I've been sensitive to it since early childhood," I explained.

I turned around, distanced myself from him, and left the building in slow steps. What a surreal experience that was.

The next day, a delegation of high-ranking army officers arrived at the factory area. They called all the remaining forced laborers out of their improvised hiding places for a roundup.

"Workers of Gustloff! We will now conduct a headcount!" declared an officer.

Two corporals sorted us in lines and counted twice.

"As of today, you will be reassigned to assist the bomb squads and engineering corps staff in identifying and safely defusing explosives and undetonated bombs from the area of the factory compound!"

The soldiers then walked through the line of prisoners and distributed dozens of giant steel shovels and buckets that came out of the army truck.

We were tasked to dig about 100 feet deep into each of the craters and retrieve bombs that failed to explode. The soldiers marked about 50 crater locations with live bombs lying in them.

They then taught us how to form traditional digger chains and divided us into task teams. The first group of diggers were positioned at the lowest level of the crater, digging deeper, and removing soil to the sides. The second group would move the soil upwards with the shovels. A third group would be placed at the top of the crater and carry the soil away. That was hard labor for all prisoners, many of whom had had little or no real food since the factory was destroyed. Some prisoners dropped to the ground out of exhaustion; others could not hold on to their shovels more than a few hours at a time.

At the end of the first workday, my group identified the first bomb, and a German bomb squad went down to defuse it. Then a

German engineering section operated a heavy crane to pull out the fuseless bomb.

The next day I was teamed up with another group, and we were also able to defuse and pull out one bomb after hours of moving soil. The remaining prisoners went into a new routine of bomb removal. There was no more armament factory to supply us with work. The camp administration conducted two roundups every day and managed the work with the engineering teams and bomb squads.

Father, are you alive? Where are you? Standing deep inside a bomb crater, dirt on my entire body, I was eager to know, but had no one to ask.

8 NESTLÉ

I was now camp prisoner Alexander from the bomb squad.

My muscles were aching from moving hundreds of pounds of gravel out of the craters during our daily bomb hunt. I sorely missed my warehouse rounds across the Mauser rifle assembly line as well as my cleaning chores and cursed at the Americans for bombing the factory and putting an end to our successful, international weapon sabotage operation. If only they knew. Would any of us ever live to tell this incredible story?

During one of the roundups, a fat, balding German officer, wearing a fancy fur coat, appeared, stepped forward, and shouted through a megaphone he held in his hand.

"Prisoners! If any of you is a skilled and trained typewriter mechanic, you must take one step forward immediately! This is an order!"

No response from the prisoners.

I was daydreaming while standing, my thoughts were completely elsewhere, and my eyes were pecking.

"Typewriter mechanic, take one step forward immediately!" repeated the officer through the megaphone.

Hearing the question clearly for the first time almost subconsciously made me reminisce about the good times during my typewriter apprenticeship days at Miloslav Schweska in Bratislava. What good days they were. Well, if there were no other volunteers, I might as well.

I took a step forward.

The fat officer and a few soldiers approached me. Two of the soldiers started kicking and hitting me, and I fell, instantly regretting my hasty decision to volunteer.

"You Jew swine, why did you let me wait and tear up my throat?" asked the officer with a disgusted look.

"I was only an apprentice! I was only an apprentice!" I screamed apologetically as they kicked me.

"Can you clean and fix typewriters?"

"Yes! Yes! Absolutely. I was a good apprentice."

They stopped kicking and escorted me away from the line.

"Wash him at once!" shouted the officer at the soldiers accompanying me. "Make him scrub off all the dirt and disease. Make him replace his disgusting, dirty clothes! Give him a new pair of shoes! Cut his hair!"

They led me to a desolate row of wooden structures, outside the perimeter of the Gustloff fence. One soldier opened the door, and we all went in.

"This is your new workspace, Jew," shouted that same soldier.

It was a rather small room, at the edge of a very elongated building. A locked door divided my space from the rest of the cabin, which was incomparably bigger. On one side of the room, there were one large desk, two chairs adjacent to the wall, and a window facing another wooden hut. On the other side of the room was a steep mountain of shattered and broken Mercedes typewriters, piled one on top of the other. Judging by their condition, I assumed they were most probably damaged during the air raids. There were dozens of them, likely accumulated from multiple regional offices and locations.

"What do you need from us to start fixing and cleaning the typewriters immediately?" asked the second soldier.

"I will kindly ask you for a mini screwdriver set sizes zero to four, a needle-nose pliers, a flat-nose pliers, a snap-ring pliers, standard detergents, a small soft brush, a small hard brush, plenty of pieces of cleaning cloth, and a large bottle of water. Thank you very much."

The soldier wrote down my wish list to the dot and read it back to me top to bottom to confirm.

"This better be the complete list, Jew. You will suffer if I need to go find you anything else later, understood?"

"This is all I need, thank you."

Once I confirmed, he left me sitting there with the other soldier, who used that window of opportunity to examine me carefully. He took me to the soldiers' showers and watched me as I cleaned up thoroughly. When I was done showering, he handed me a new pair of prisoner uniform and a new pair of shoes. He apologized that the barber would only be able to see me the following day. I obviously didn't fuss about it. We went back to my new typewriter studio.

Minutes later, the first soldier came back with literally everything I had asked for.

"Can you confirm you have received everything you have asked for, Jew?"

Order must be kept, even in the most awkward of situations. How German of him.

"I hereby confirm, sir," I replied formally after carefully going through the items, to his evident satisfaction.

The soldiers then introduced me to Hans, an older German man wearing a soldier's uniform, who was temporarily assigned to guard me. The old timer could barely walk, and I wasn't sure he could see more than three feet ahead through his thick spectacles.

"Nice to meet you, Hans. My name is Alexander. I will not cause you any trouble," I introduced myself.

"Very well," said Hans and sat down. The two other soldiers left.

On my second day on the job, the fat, balding officer who picked me out from the roundup came to inspect my work. Apparently, he was an avid fan of machines, analog devices in general, and German typewriters in particular. He wished to be positively certain that I indeed knew what I was doing.

As I learned during my apprenticeship days, Mercedes typewriters had one big advantage for technicians. By removing only two side screws, the entire typewriter keyboard could be disassembled. Moreover, the carriage return lever was much more easily discharged compared to other types of typewriters, namely American ones such as Remington or Smith Corona. Consequently, I was easily able to demonstrate to the fat, balding officer how I successfully assembled a totally dismantled Mercedes typewriter within a few seconds.

"Young boy, you are by no means an apprentice. You are a proper master." The officer was genuinely impressed.

"Sir, if you also wished for me to polish and make the machines spotless and looking brand new, I would need a container of gasoline, engine oil, and some grease." I tried to build some momentum from my unexpected success.

Everything I asked for was brought to my desk within the hour.

After half a day of work, in which I took apart, assembled, fixed, spotlessly cleaned, and oiled it, the first refurbished Mercedes typewriter was ready to be presented and reassigned to the German Army. It looked completely brand new. The officer was so gleeful, I was sure he was about to kiss me. Or maybe even worse.

"What a talented pair of hands you have, my boy!" He was ecstatic. "May I bring you something, anything, to eat? How can I make your work more enjoyable and comfortable?" he asked. "We truly appreciate your service."

That was now the second senior German official who had engaged in pretend play, assuming that we were an employee and a boss, and providing professional feedback. I found it completely ridiculous. *Should I be asking for an end-of-year bonus?*

"May I ask for your name, Mr. Officer?"

"I am Major Maximilian Steiger, and you may address me as Major Steiger."

"Thank you, Major Steiger. You have been very kind to me. I have all the food and supplies I require to fulfill your orders and requirements in a satisfactory manner, sir."

"Very well. I shall visit you again tomorrow, then." He took his bow and left the hut.

Hans, witnessing the lovefest between the senior officer and Jewish prisoner, was visibly impressed.

"Where did you learn your trade, boy?" Hans asked. "I thought all Jews were useless with their hands."

"I was a locksmith apprentice as a young child in my hometown in Czechoslovakia. I then worked as a technician apprentice in Bratislava before I was captured and sent here."

"Hmm. And where did you pick up such flawless, rich German?"

"We practically grew up educated as Germans. We mainly spoke German at home, sir. My grandparents only spoke German to us. I had a German tutor who visited me every day. I have been reading classic German authors for as long as I can remember."

"Hmm. Very impressive."

"If I may ask sir, what did you do before the war?"

"We are a family of farmers from Bavaria. Both my sons died on the Eastern Front. Last year they forced everyone under the age of 65 to volunteer to the *Wehrmacht*, so I did. Since then, I've been here, a guard at this camp."

"My condolences for the loss of your sons. We have also lost many family members. I hope the war ends soon so you and I can go back home to our families and rebuild our lives."

"Same to you. I pray to God every day."

Every time I had to walk out to bring in additional technical supplies or to visit the latrine, Hans would accompany me. It was now strictly forbidden for prisoners to walk into, or around the area of the bombed factory. Hans and I would stroll around the wreckage, near the demolished, old dispensary building and supply center, to scout for cleaning materials and pieces of cloth.

In only a few days, I managed to build myself a small, well-equipped, and neat workshop. It became evident to me that this small workshop was an important part in the process of repairing the communications, control, and command centers that had been badly damaged during the last air raid.

On the one hand, my quality of life vastly improved overnight after that pivotal roundup. I had all the food I could eat. They brought me leftovers from the soldiers' kitchen, and I tasted cooked vegetables and pork for the first time in many months. I was allowed to walk around the camp unharmed and freely, with Hans.

On the other hand, they kept me awake for most of the first nights, to enhance my ability to do my job. After my first all-nighter, I was able to hand over five refurbished Mercedes machines. Major Steiger could not believe his eyes. To show his gratitude, he started supplying an ever-growing number of damaged units. My workload improved in the following days, and I was able to get back to my fellow prisoners some nights and get some proper sleep.

Father was on my mind constantly. I still hadn't heard a word about his fate. Was he being medically treated in Buchenwald? Was he badly hurt? Was he released back to the Small Camp and now fighting for his own survival, staying outdoors during the freezing nights?

My only two powerful contacts in camp were Günter and Major Steiger. The former disappeared, vanished off the face of the earth, and I feared he had died during the air raid. I didn't have the confidence to approach Major Steiger with any personal requests yet. I knew I needed to build some more trust before asking for his help with Father.

Nevertheless, my confidence levels were building by the day.

One morning and without prior notice, Hans stopped showing up. No one mentioned anything to me, and I didn't bother asking. No other guard was assigned to me during my time in the workshop. I

116

was a free prisoner again, only escorted to and from the improvised sleeping quarters.

I was left to my own devices in my private typewriter refurbishing office but made sure that I didn't lower my guard. They could be watching me. Someone could be here any second. I couldn't risk it. After a week had elapsed and no soldiers were in sight, other than to deliver food, I felt that the danger level had subsided. I could no longer suppress my curiosity and just had to know what was behind the locked door in my room.

I would stare at the door and imagine the contents of that gigantic, forbidden hall behind it. One day, it contained boatloads of files, detailing the whereabouts of Jewish prisoners throughout Europe. Going through the indexes, I found where Mother was sent to, and copied her personal information and location. Another day, it held vast medicinal cabinets containing drugs, vaccines, and bandages. I located stashes of vitamins and put myself on a wellness regime, nurturing my body back to form, so I could save Father. What were the Germans actually hiding there?

Using my tool kit, which now also included a heavy hammer, assorted metal pieces, and myriad strings I had collected outside, I built a thief's jimmy: a thin crowbar I could use to easily unlock the door.

Food was delivered clockwise, at pre-set times twice a day, and the refurbished machines were picked up every day, at the end of the workday. I did not fear being surprised by unannounced visitors.

Waiting until my meal was delivered, I made sure the soldiers were out of sight. It was 11 o'clock in the morning and there was not a living soul within hundreds of yards. It was time to break into the inner door. My jimmy worked like it was supposed to, and the door opened almost instantly.

I found myself standing inside a huge, unlit warehouse. The only light came from my typewriter atelier's window. My small office was the backroom for this expansive storage space. I could only see the back of the last row of large, heavy-looking carton parcels. All the boxes had the English words "Red Cross" printed in giant letters on them.

What could those boxes contain? My curiosity was peaking.

Using a piece of metal, I tore through one of the boxes. Inside, I saw dozens of flat, brown Nestlé chocolate bars. *No, this wasn't really happening.* I closed my eyes, counted to three, and then opened them again. The Nestlé bars were still there, and it was no dream. The same cardboard container also contained sealed jars containing instant coffee, crates of waffles, and bags of sugar and milk powder. My eyes refocused on the chocolates.

That afternoon, I stuffed my face with more chocolate than I had eaten during my entire, young life.

I was now Aladdin in the treasure cave.

Apparently, the Germans located my makeshift workshop in the same building where they were secretly hiding confiscated stashes of the International Red Cross relief shipments, probably targeted to reach the Allied Forces' prisoners of war in Buchenwald and elsewhere. The Germans impounded the parcels, and hid them in a godforsaken wooden shed, near a small village. The young Jewish prisoner entered that secret hiding place like a mouse would, from the dark corner of the back door side. The parcels I opened were situated in the last cabinet of a long shed, whose entrance was on the opposite side of the entrance to my workshop. Any person looking at the boxes from the front of the cabinet would not be aware that a mouse had torn them open and feasted on the Nestlé bars. They couldn't catch me. When I was done collecting my daily chocolate quota, I would do my best to conceal the rupture in the parcels, just in case.

I had hit the jackpot. I had the winning numbers in an unlevel playing field. Once again, I had leverage, but who knows for how long? I needed to use that leverage immediately to find Father.

It didn't make sense to bring any of the Red Cross goodies back to the sleeping barracks. An informant would sell me out to the Germans in five seconds. However, my close comrades there were practically starving while I was sitting on the mother lode, my lips dripping with sugar. I took a number of chocolate bars and walked back guarded to the Gustloff compound that evening.

"Zdeněk, come here for a second," I said. "Here, take and hide these, quickly. After you eat them, you must bury the wrappings in the ground."

He almost fainted when he saw the two Nestlé bars I had shoved into the palm of his hand.

"But, but how?"

"Don't tell a soul, but the Germans are giving me these treats to show their appreciation for my loyal work. I will get you more."

He hugged me and ran to his bunk to swallow the chocolates. I feared he might choke, but he was fine. He had a big smile on his face that entire evening.

I also gave two bars to Christophe, who responded in similar fashion. I decided to only share my good fortune with people I trusted wholeheartedly, and there were only two of them.

A chance had been given to me to find out where Father was. In this godforsaken land, I was practically the only dealer in the market with hard currency, in the form of chocolate in massive quantities, within a radius of many kilometers. *How do I handle this trade?* Coming up with the right execution plan was key. I spent long hours at the workshop, considering my options and coming up with a strategy. It was a long shot, but those were dark days, and long shots were hard to come by.

My plan relied on two pillars.

The first was cultural. Even when times were really challenging and unprecedented, the Germans made sure immaculate order was kept. At any given point, the camp's administration would have an updated card index on every inmate in the Buchenwald region. The information about Father's whereabouts was undoubtedly there, updated, accurate, and accessible.

The second was logistical. The camp worked like a well-oiled machine, where the same people conducted the same tasks day after day, in a predictable and repeatable pattern. I had carefully studied and learned the daily arrival and departure schedule of the food supply trucks, coming from the main camp in Buchenwald. Every morning, I saw the same Kapo who accompanied the driver. Like many of them, this Kapo was a German-speaking Jew and I believed I could easily communicate with him. He had seen me walking alongside Major Steiger on a couple of occasions, speaking perfect German, and was exposed to my unique position in the camp. He was the best access key I could positively identify.

One morning, I approached him and stood very close to his face.

"My dear sir, as you know, I work for Major Steiger. Stefan Ružiak, my father, was taken away from Gustloff after the bombing for medical treatment in Buchenwald. His prisoner number is 98663. If you can locate him, you shall have this," and I took out and flashed a shiny, sealed bar of Nestlé chocolate and slowly raised it in front of his face.

The Kapo's eyes nearly popped out of their sockets, and he started breathing heavily.

"This is impossible. Where did you get this?" he asked, shell-shocked.

"Well, just between us Jews, you know how the Germans love me and how important my technical skills are to their war effort. They reward me with many types of perks, like this chocolate bar, but not only," I answered nonchalantly.

I wrote Father's prisoner number on a piece of paper and handed it to the Kapo.

We had a deal.

The Kapo took the piece of paper, and the truck drove away back to camp.

A sleepless night at the barracks followed. Was the Kapo greedy enough to cooperate? Will he sell me out? Was this my last day as a pseudo-free, entrepreneurial prisoner? Will the Kapo lead me to Father? Overall, I had a good feeling about the next day.

The truck was back the next morning, and I immediately knew the answer.

From my vantage point inside the workshop, I could see the excited Kapo looking around impatiently. He was undoubtedly seeking me, waiting to collect on his chocolate bar.

I came outside to greet him.

"I found your father. Show me my chocolate now."

My hand reached into my pocket and let the bar peek out.

"The administration index indicates that your father belongs to Block 29."

"Good job, kind sir, this belongs to you," I said, handing over the earned wage.

The Kapo hurried to conceal the bar under his coat.

Moving on to stage two of my plan.

That afternoon in the workshop, I wrote the letter.

Father, this is Sanyi. I am alive and well. How are you doing? Please reply on the back of this paper and hand it to the person who delivered it to you. He can be trusted.

Remembering the Kapo's excitement upon seeing the first chocolate bar, I figured this next step would be a walk in the park.

The following morning, I went to see the Kapo who had arrived on the truck.

"Do you want two other bars?" I asked, waving them in front of the Kapo. "You will have them once you return with a written answer from Stefan Ružiak in Block 29."

I handed over the letter and we had ourselves another deal.

The next day, I had two fewer chocolate bars, but was holding a handwritten letter from Father.

"My dearest Sanyi, how happy I am to know you are alive! I'm hanging in there, very thin, with hardly any strength left. Please come for me. Dad."

I knew then and there that I would see him again.

The war developments were shifting the situation around the camp quickly. It was the beginning of April, and we started hearing around-the-clock battle noises and understood that the front was inching closer every day, and that the Germans were nearing their inevitable defeat. There were explosions, cannon fire, light artillery, and even small arms fire. Unsurprisingly, a few days later the Germans decided to evacuate all the prisoners from the smaller, adjacent camps, back into Buchenwald.

Major Steiger visited me the morning before.

"My young Alexander, this is your last day in the workshop. Tomorrow, all the contents of the workshop, including the remaining damaged machines, will be transferred to the Main Camp and I will contact you once you are back and settled in to set you up in a new location, so you can continue this important work. In the meantime, please finish as many machines as you can today."

"Yes, Major Steiger. Please allow me to spend the night here so I can handle as many machines as possible."

"Of course, my child. The truck will pick you up outside in the morning."

My time in the Nestlé Kingdom had come to an end. Only a few hours left next to my precious stash of hard currency. No time to lose.

That night I worked on as many typewriters as I could fix, and filled my clothes, pants, shirt, and coat with as many as 20 chocolate bars. I used a long thin rope to secure them tightly and made sure they didn't fall and were not visible when I walked.

The next morning, all the remaining prisoners from the Gustloff compound area, about 1,000 feeble men, arrived at Buchenwald. Anyone observing our marching group would easily spot that one prisoner looked noticeably healthier and heavier than the rest, his coat puffed and swollen. Actually, after my recent chocolate consumption spree, that day I was stronger and carried more body weight than most teenagers I knew before the war. Zdeněk and I walked together, and we went through almost the identical reception process that Father and I had gone through upon arrival to the camp almost six months earlier.

We formed lines, and our numbers and details were updated into the card indexes. When registration was complete, the block commanders arrived to gather as many prisoners as each block could handle and fit. All I could think of was Block 29. I was waiting for that number to be called. One after the other, block commanders came and left with groups of prisoners. There were not many of us left standing there, and I was still waiting.

Block 29 was never called out. *How could that be?*

Did the Kapo lie about Father's whereabouts? If so, how had he managed to provide a letter from Father, in his familiar handwriting? Something didn't add up.

Zdeněk tried to persuade me that we should join one of the other groups.

"Don't be stupid," he said. "Obviously, there is no Block 29. You'll be left without a block."

"But I *know* he is in Block 29. He wrote me a letter himself from there!"

"Alex, you won't find him today. Please come with me, and we will continue looking for him tomorrow."

He was right. Reluctantly, I joined him and the last group leaving the roll call ground.

The block we were allocated to in the Main Camp was crammed with people. It was divided into a nighttime sleeping space and a daytime space, furnished with a few chairs and a fireplace. While peak winter was behind us, it was still rather cold, especially at night. The prisoners would all crowd inside, as close as possible to the fireplace, to keep warm.

Conditions there were incomparable to our wretched existence in the Small Camp before being shipped to Gustloff. Still, six prisoners had to share every bunk bed, three in the upper level and three down in the bottom level. Watery soup was the only food our captors served here. The block Kapo would order us to leave the sleeping space in the morning and only allowed us to enter back in the afternoon.

I started speaking with the Kapo during one of the soup queues, and within a few days he already knew who I was. I only had one trick, tried and true, literally up my sleeve. It worked well twice, and the time arrived to give it a third test.

After lunch, I asked to speak to the Kapo outside the block.

"Would you be interested in receiving a most tasty Nestlé chocolate bar?" I asked, looking directly into the man's eyes.

"You miserable idiot, you must be hallucinating due to malnutrition. Leave me alone. I don't believe you and don't have time for this nonsense," answered the Kapo.

"I thought you might say that. Here is one piece from your bar, enjoy it." I handed him a chocolate cube.

He examined the piece of chocolate, smelled it twice, and put it in his mouth. He then broke into tears and immediately dried his face with his sleeve.

"I want the chocolate bar, give it to me now," he said.

"The rest of the bar is yours if you help me. My father is held in Block 29. I suspect he is probably very sick. I know he's alive as he recently sent me a letter. I want to see him at once."

"Block 29 is a confined, isolated block, sealed with barbed wire, only housing the severely wounded and ill," said the Kapo.

It was now clear why no Kapo had called out that block number at the roll call ground when we arrived at camp.

The Kapo was contemplating his next move. He examined me closely.

"Come with me," he said after a few seconds.

Without hesitation, the Kapo started walking away from our block, with me lagging not far behind.

It was a beautiful, sunny day, as we approached a large, rectangular yard, surrounded by a barbed-wire fence. On the inner side, prisoners who were well enough to stand and walk were slowly nearing the fence when they saw us coming.

Father was nowhere to be seen.

"I will give you two chocolate bars if we find him and bring him back with us," I said, upping the ante.

My soft, confident tone and the apparent abundance of chocolate supply at the heart of a German concentration camp overwhelmed the puzzled Kapo, but he said nothing.

"Follow me."

We walked into the yard of Block 29. Experienced from my past quest to find Father, all I was looking for were shiny white coat buttons.

A man wearing a dark coat with white buttons was leaning on the block wall. He didn't look anything like my father, but I immediately knew it was him. That man was the thinnest adult I have ever seen. He couldn't have weighed more than 75 pounds, just flesh and bones. They used to call the living corpses in the camp *Muselmänner*, because their feeble leg muscles would not allow them to stand and they were typically found in a prone position, resembling Muslim men praying. My father was now a *Muselmann*.

Father started limping towards the fence, and the Kapo and I began walking towards him. I hugged his fragile body carefully. "I'm here, Father, you are safe. I will take care of you now."

"Sanyi, my dear child, I knew you would come. It is too late; it is too late," he muttered and continued, "I don't know if I have much time left. I wished to see you before I die." He started fading while trying to pronounce his last sentence.

"You will be just fine. I promised Mother we will both make it back safe and sound, and I intend to keep my promise because I'm scared of Mother, just as much as you are. She will kill me if you die. Have mercy on me. She will kill you too!"

He gave a weak smile, and I knew he had the strength in him to fight on.

The Kapo went into the block and came out five minutes later with the signed, formal transfer paper for Stefan Ružiak, turning him over to our block.

The three partners in crime – Father, the Kapo, and I – started heading back to our block. On the way, I slipped two bars into the

Kapo's open hand. Father was leaning on me and walking very slowly.

A rule was then publicly broken. In front of the curious eyes of all the block prisoners, the Kapo and I led Father into the sleeping space during daytime. We lifted one of the beds and made space under it for him to lie down. The Kapo left us alone, and I took out a chocolate bar and slowly started feeding it to him. His head was working just fine, his thoughts crystal clear. Alas, his body was crushed and broken. In the evening, when the soup quota was distributed, the Kapo gave me a double portion, so I could feed Father. He started regaining his strength slowly, hour by hour.

The sounds of battle, machine gun, air bombings, and cannon fire, were getting louder, and seemingly closer, every day. The undeniable scent of the German Army's defeat was felt all around. We were hopeful but had no idea what that defeat would spell for us, when it finally arrived. The German personnel's body language testified to the soldiers' fear and anxiety. They knew the end of their war was coming. Would they end us together with them?

I didn't hear from or see Major Steiger again. Apparently, my glory days as a typewriter apprentice at the service of the Third Reich were behind me. Oh, well.

9 PORK DINNER

After days of careful feeding that consisted of soup with chocolate cubes, Father started regaining his facial color and physical form. He started looking like himself again. His body began building a thin layer of fat and some muscle mass. I forced him to go on short walks with me to enhance his stamina. The first day, he couldn't walk for more than a couple of minutes. The next day, our afternoon stroll lasted ten minutes. All my focus and time were dedicated to making him feel better.

"Sanyi, check out all the trucks and cars." He pointed towards the main administration building as we were walking around the yard. "Something is definitely going on. I think they are waving the white flag and preparing to flee."

We stopped our turtle-pace walk, and our eyes started following the German Army movements. Officers and soldiers were carrying large document boxes, loading them and getting into the vehicles, and speeding out of the camp.

"Are they really leaving the camp right now?" I couldn't believe both my eyes and my words. "Is this the German Army running for its life?"

"I still can't believe it," he said with a suspect expression. "Let's be very careful. Let's lower our profile and wait inside. Please walk me back."

We went back into the block. The regular soup portion was served on time for dinner. We couldn't see a single Gestapo or German soldier walking around the block that evening. We could clearly see the guards up in their tower positions, so I couldn't make sense of what was really happening. The camp was not fully deserted of our captors yet.

Explosion noises were heard constantly.

The next day was April 11, 1945. We were awakened by loud sounds of artillery rounds. Otherwise, everything was very quiet, but the guards were still up there with their metal helmets, aiming their rifles outward.

In the early afternoon, out of the blue, it was all over. Camp Buchenwald had fallen.

We suddenly saw all the German guards hastily climb down from the watchtowers. A single tank broke through the main steel gate, dragging it under its chains, and halted in the middle of the camp, close to our block. The charging tank was swiftly followed by ground troops. Our deepest wishes were answered.

"Father, the soldiers are here; the Germans are fleeing!" I started shouting.

"Are the soldiers Russians or Americans? Please, please, let them be Americans!" he exclaimed, unable to hide his excitement and anxiety.

I looked more closely. "I think they are Americans!" I shouted, having seen the letter markings on the tank.

He sat down on the ground, holding his head. He was crying and laughing at the same time.

Guards were running amok all around us, but no one was noticing them anymore. Just in front of me, a young German guard threw down his rifle, dropped his ammunition kit, and took off his helmet and army shirt, as he was passing me by. He was hoping to blend into the prisoners, but I doubt he managed to. I didn't really care, as all I wanted to do was to touch the tank and know that this moment was real.

"Stay here, Father. Go rest in your bed in the bunk. I will be back for you. I'm going to see the American tank."

I ran towards the Sherman. Together with me was a herd of prisoners, the ones who could carry themselves, circling it. We were shouting, cheering, crying, calling, whistling. It was chaotic. It was the most beautiful chaos one could imagine. We felt we could lift that steel monster up in the air with our bare hands.

Two GIs emerged from the belly of the tank and sat on the turret. Nothing prepared them to be greeted like Greek gods by thousands of half-living, half-dead, skin-and-bone survivors. I squeezed through the crowd and made it to the tank. My hand shakily lifted to feel the hot steel.

"Mother! Mother! We are coming! Can you hear me?" I shouted in Hungarian.

A young American soldier sitting two feet above my head was listening to my screams and looking at me with a wide smile, amused. He obviously didn't understand a word I was saying. I formed the universal thank-you signal placing both my hands on my heart and bowed my head. He bowed back. That was my cue to leave the tank and rush back to Father.

Dozens of American troops were now storming into camp by foot. There was not a German in sight anymore.

After six months of captivity, famine, freezing cold, and torture, we were free, along with tens of thousands of survivors around us. But we were also sick, dying, hungry, and discombobulated. We now just sat on our bunk beds and waited for something to happen, and someone to tell us what to do.

Within a few hours, the camp's new commanders started making their presence felt. "Everybody out, the American officer is here to explain the new situation," shouted the block Kapo.

The bunks emptied slowly.

A young Yankee officer wearing a cap was standing in front of us in the yard. He had a German interpreter standing next to him. "On behalf of the Sixth Armored Division of the United States Army and the Allies, I am happy to tell you that the Buchenwald concentration camp was liberated today. The German Army is gone. You are all free men now," said the officer, followed by the interpreter.

Some of the prisoners were clapping. We were eagerly waiting to hear what else the American had to say. How soon could Father see a doctor? How soon could he eat some meat or vegetables? How soon could we leave? I assumed the officer was going between the blocks and conveying a generic message, and that it would take a long while before my questions were answered.

"Our battalion, and additional adjacent units, were given responsibility over this camp. We are here to help you heal and recover. Our teams are preparing to receive shipments of food and medicine for you..."

"How will they be able to take care of all these thousands of dying men?" I asked in a low voice, not expecting a reply.

"...Doctors will be coming to examine you in the coming hours," he continued. "We ask that only the ones that are most in need see the doctors today. When you see aid vehicles, please do not proceed towards them. We kindly ask that you stay in your block. I assure you all, everyone will get the food and medical care they deserve and need..."

"When are we getting our soup? I'm hungry," whispered Father.

"I don't know. With everything's that happened, I don't know if the kitchen is operating right now," I whispered back. "These Americans better get their act together quickly, or we'll surely starve. Also, we are all out of Nestlé chocolate."

"... Our medical unit has already emptied an adjacent block and turned it into a field hospital. We will be transferring the severely ill and weak for immediate treatment there..."

"Father, you will stay with me in this block. I will take care of you."

"Yes."

"... A temporary large-scale kitchen has been opened in the main camp building and we will resume regular meal service within the hour."

"Hallelujah!"

A doctor and his medical staff came into our block later that night. He examined Father and was content with his pulse and blood pressure. He didn't suggest transferring him to the hospital. I guess there were thousands of *Muselmänner* who were doing far worse than he was. He had Nestlé to thank for that.

We all received warmer, new clothes.

Trucks started driving in, loaded with hundreds of pigs and dozens of chickens. The noise the animals made was ear-piercing. Jews represented a minority of camp inmates, so eating pork meat, the most common form of protein in that area, was not an issue for most. However, many of the starving Jewish prisoners refused the non-kosher dishes.

"Did the Americans rob a zoo?" I asked the Kapo who was standing next to me, half-joking.

"Word is that they went through all nearby villages and confiscated everything. And I mean everything. Now we'll see who's going to starve." The cheery Kapo sounded vengeful.

The smell of cooked meat spread around the camp like a cloud and mesmerized all inhabitants. The American commanders had only the best of intentions, but their ill-planned feast would lead to a terrible human calamity. The fatty pork plates that were served in the block that evening caused dozens of deaths. The *Muselmänner*, who were lying in bunks in groups of five all around us and had lost most of their body weight, could not digest all that meat. Many of them died following this celebratory dinner.

When Father saw the meat plate, he went completely berserk.

"Feed me, please!" He started shivering.

The smell of burnt pig fat drove his senses mad. I resisted. "Eating this whole portion is very bad for you. Your body can't handle it yet. I will cut very small pieces and feed you one by one. Please be very patient with me. We will do this all night if needed."

I placed miniscule bits of nonfatty meat in his mouth. We spent about three hours digesting just a few small pieces of meat. Father felt fine after that dinner.

The next day we started seeing members of the international press, journalists, and photographers walking around the camp. One of them entered our block and walked between the bunks. He was covering his nose and mouth with a piece of cloth, nauseated by the concoction of stenches coming from the humans inside, dead and alive. A few young, energized inmates circled him and tried to lift him on their shoulders. They were too weak to hold him, although the journalist wasn't heavy. He walked between the bunks, attempting to decipher and translate the scenes in front of him. He was utterly shocked, speaking to a microphone connected to a large recording device. He and his cameraman were accompanied by army press officers and doctors who were explaining the living conditions and situations in the bunk and camp. I felt like a monkey in a zoo.

Later we were all invited to participate in personal interviews. I sat in front of an American civilian who conducted the session in English, through a German interpreter, and took notes.

"What is your name?"

"Alexander Ružiak. Originally Alexander Rosenberg, but we falsified our names when we went into hiding in Slovakia."

"What is your prisoner number?"

"98662."

"What is your date of birth?"

"November 2, 1927."

"What is your place of birth?"

"Sečovce, Czechoslovakia."

"When did you arrive at Buchenwald? Where from?"

"Arrived from Sachsenhausen about six months ago."

"When and where were you captured?"

"Captured in Bratislava. Transferred to Sachsenhausen through Nováky, shortly before arriving at Buchenwald."

"Have you been employed as a forced laborer?"

"Yes."

"Have you been a victim of violence and / or abuse?"

"Yes." I provided detailed descriptions of our experiences.

"You are free to go, Alexander."

"Just a minute, please. Would you be able to look up your files and see if you know the whereabouts of my mother, Irena Rosenberg, or Irena Ružiak, who was also captured with us in Bratislava?"

"Unfortunately, no. You can go now. Take care and good luck. Oh, and one more thing. This afternoon, if you are up for it, you should come out of the block and gather along the fence. We are marching the local town people and villagers to visit the camp, see what they've been supporting all these years."

"Oh, very interesting. Thank you."

Leaving the interview room, I received a Certificate of Liberation, proof that I was indeed on the inside of the Buchenwald barbed-wire fence when that tank broke through on April 11. I helped Father attend his interview and picked up his certificate as well.

And indeed, that afternoon, we played the roles of animals in the zoo for the local population, in what the Americans saw as an educational imperative. They ordered all the remaining residents of Weimar to walk down the 17 kilometers leading to Buchenwald, to witness the Nazi horrors with their own eyes. And what an experience it was for them.

They saw the hundreds of skinny corpses in the center of camp, and the lines of *Muselmänner* staring at them from behind the fence. The engineering unit waited until the civilians were in place to bring about three giant bulldozers to dig mass graves and shove the dead bodies into them. Those young German kids would never be able to get that sight out of their heads.

They smelled the unbearable stench of death and disease.

They held onto the steel-wired fence that separated the camp from the world outside. They didn't feel the freezing cold on their skins, because it was a beautiful Thuringian early spring day.

I stood close to the gate and looked at the German men, women, and children who stood on the other side. They looked poor and beaten, albeit better fed than us.

Suddenly, out of the crowd, came a shout. "Lexa! Lexa! It's me! Lexa!"

I recognized the voice instantly, and almost instinctively reached out to pick up an invisible cleaning detergent container. It was Günter, standing alongside the other people of Weimar. The bastard was alive. He looked well and was visibly excited to see me.

I walked closer and stood in front of him, on the other side of the fence.

"I'm so happy to see that you are alive, Lexa. I didn't know if you survived the air raid, and we were not allowed to go back to the factory afterwards. You must believe me! I wanted to go back and help my people. Such a human tragedy. Is... is Stefan alive?" he asked.

"Yes, he is, just barely. Thank you for asking."

Using his hands, he signaled that he wanted me to bring my ear closer to the fence. I was now standing a few centimeters away from him.

"Lexa, I need your help. Please." He spoke in a low voice. "You know that I have always treated Stefan and you well. I saved his life when he was suspected of aiding the escapees. I saved your life when the soldier was about to break your body during the selection process in camp. You must help me now. You will be asked to sign a paper saying that I was good to you and to Stefan, and that you never saw me mistreat a factory worker. Otherwise, the Americans will put me to trial and hang me."

"Of course, I will sign it, Günter. You have been good to us. You have been good to other workers. I'm happy to see you are alive."

He smiled at me. "I knew you would. I will be back in a day or two and ask to see you," he concluded and bid me farewell.

I didn't tell Father about my encounter with Günter that day. I never saw Günter again and don't know what happened to him. It wouldn't surprise me to hear that he was lynched by his former prisoners. That thought didn't shock me, despite my sympathy towards him. The war was strange that way. We heard of numerous acts of revenge in the days following liberation.

"Are we allowed to leave?" asked Father that evening.

"I don't know. I don't think so. They haven't published any transportation or evacuation plans."

"So? What's preventing us from going home?"

"For one, you can't travel yet. You are sick and weak, and your body will not survive the train trip. We will stay in the camp until the doctors say you are well enough to travel."

I made sure that Father received medical treatment and proper food and gave him time to gather his strengths.

The American doctor who took care of him made Father feel as if the Free World's future hinged on Solomon Rosenberg's ability to gain weight.

"Climb the scales, Zoli. I like our chances this morning. I want to see we gained at least two pounds."

Father stood on the instrument.

"Fantastic, Zoli! One hundred and seven pounds! This is progress! We are building strength. Continue taking your daily walks with your son, eating our chef's culinary delights, and taking the vitamins I gave you. I assure you that our food does not include the bromide that these asshole Germans made you eat."

That was news to me. "Bromide? What are you talking about?"

"Did you ever hear your father, yourself or other prisoners say that they lost their desire to live?"

"Oh, only every day," I answered.

"Well, it's likely that the chemical bromide that was put in your soup was to some extent the reason for that. That chemical causes people to lose any hope or desire to live."

If I had any ability to feel further disgust towards the Nazis, I probably would have.

A few days after the liberation, the US Army placed in the center of the camp large boards with daily updated lists of survivor names from all other concentration and extermination camps in Europe. I went there after each update to look for the names of Mother and other family members on the board.

"Anything on the board?" he asked daily.

"Nothing," I answered daily.

We did not know if Mother, or any other member of our family, was alive. We were bracing ourselves for bad news, or even worse, no news at all. Lowering expectations had proven to be our best defense mechanism during the war.

It was springtime in Buchenwald. I found interest in improving my English by chatting with random US soldiers around the camp. There was always someone on a cigarette break, willing to spend ten minutes teaching me new vocabulary.

Otherwise, I was bored laying around the block all day and started contemplating post-camp life. We had no civilian clothes, no money, no home to go back to. Did we have a country to go back to? I wasn't sure if Mother or any other family members were alive, and so our destination was not at all obvious. For any option we opted for, we needed money.

How could a young, entrepreneurial, son-of-a-trader survivor make a quick buck while still under military rule, albeit a friendly one? At the heels of a world war, I figured looting would be an acceptable option. While I wasn't very comfortable with the morality of the act, I'd be stealing from the people who killed my family members and neighbors and, on a number of occasions, tried to kill me, and took away all of our belongings. I could live with that.

So, I started wandering around and outside the camp, now a free, unencumbered man. Around the camp's perimeter, beyond the gates, stood houses where German soldiers used to live with their families until the liberation. They had all either died, fled, or been captured. Most of the houses were deserted, and I visited many of them. They were generally empty, as many visited them before I did, and took anything of value.

In one of the houses, I encountered a heavy, locked, metal door. It was no match for the locksmith apprentice from Sečovce. The door gave way after only a few minutes of tinkering. Inside was a wonderful optical laboratory, probably built by a local amateur astronomer. In the room were dozens of lenses and telescopes of various sizes. After enjoying some stargazing, I cherry-picked three long lenses that looked the most valuable, hung them with leather straps around my neck, and left the house after making sure nobody had seen me. I locked the door to make sure no one else could share that prize with me. I entered a concentration camp looking like a telescope dealer, seeking a trade.

Five minutes into my lens tour de force, an American serviceman approached me enthusiastically. I didn't understand a word he said, and he had to find another soldier to interpret.

"How did you get these Zeiss telescopic lenses? I would really love to buy them from you. What would you like for them?"

The unwitting corporal saw in front of him a meager prisoner, and didn't know he had encountered Alexander Rosenberg, scion to the Rosenberg trader clan.

"Oh, these belonged to my beloved grandmother who recently passed, I hid them when we were captured and was now able to dig them out."

"Name your price! I have US dollar currency on me."

"If my father found out I sold his inheritance, he'll give me a Gestapo Special. I don't think I can sell them to you unfortunately."

The American was half-amused, half-excited at the prospect of closing a deal. "Here's five American dollars, that's all I have."

"I really shouldn't, I'm sorry," I said as I started walking away.

The soldier deliberated. "Seven dollars. I'll throw in this box full of candy and chocolates as well."

"My grandmother was special to me; she wouldn't want me to sell her lenses. I'm sorry."

"Ten dollars. And the sweets. That's as high as I would go."

"I'll sell it for 12, plus the sweets. Just please, don't tell my father."

"We have a deal, friend." He handed over the cash, an army candy box, and a brown bag with military chocolates, and I handed over the lenses and collected the payment.

"Your secret is safe with me," he promised.

"My grandmother had a few more of those. Would you be interested?"

"I sure would be."

"Should we meet here tomorrow, same time?"

"Done."

By the same time on the following day, I had delivered three additional lenses and was in possession of 20 US dollars, four pounds sterling, and a whole bunch of candy in my pockets.

In the following days, I sold additional optical equipment to American soldiers until there was nothing left to trade. I was now carrying a good deal of western hard currency for our upcoming trip, to whatever destination. Then I became bored again.

Roaming the abandoned village nearby, I wandered into a makeshift carpentry workshop. Inside were a group of Russian prisoners, engaged in woodworking.

"Good day, gentlemen. My name is Alexander. Do any of you know Grischa or Vladimir who used to work at Gustloff until the great air raid? I am their friend."

"We don't," said one of them. "Sorry. There are many Grischas and Vladimirs among us. We worked in a different factory. My name is Sergey."

"That's a shame. I really wanted to find them and hope they are alive. What are you doing here? Why are you not leaving the camp?"

"Probably the same as you. Bored. Found this place by chance and we're passing time while we figure out how to get back home. Misha here is an expert carpenter by trade, and he is teaching us fancy woodworking." He pointed at a prisoner who was working on building a small wooden box. It was beautifully detailed.

"Do you mind if I stayed and joined your master classes?"

"Not at all, be our guest."

I spent five days learning carpentry from a Russian virtuoso with hands of gold. He taught me about woodcutting, carving, and finishing. With his help, I created an ornate cigarette holder, my ultimate Buchenwald camp memento. Inscribed inside it, using a rubber stamp I prepared, were the word KLB, the date, and my prisoner number, 98662.

Father was looking much better by then. He was consistently gaining weight and had reacquired his famous positive attitude. He was still significantly underweight, though. Three weeks after the tank first crushed the camp gates, he was ready to join me on the trip back home.

So long, Buchenwald. May you burn to the ground.

10 BRATISLAVA II

Beyond Father's poor physical condition, there were also other, political reasons preventing us from leaving the camp immediately after liberation. During those frantic early days, as the war was raging on and a final showdown in Berlin was brewing, a debate was taking place between the Allies and the Soviet Union regarding the division of the now-occupied Third Reich. Consequently, it became difficult to arrange large-scale transportation of refugees to various regions in Europe. There wasn't anything the prisoners could do about it, so we all just sat tight until the powers managed to figure things out.

Finally, our liberators announced that they would discharge Buchenwald prisoners from the Slovakia region on American military trucks traveling to Pilsen. They chose that destination because the city was controlled by the friendly Czechs. In Pilsen, we were to be placed on a special train headed to Bratislava.

With little fanfare or celebrations, we climbed aboard the American truck on a sunny morning in May 1945. We had little more than the clothes on our backs. In a small bag, I kept our certificates, candy, wooden cigarette case, and the money I had made through trades. As the truck drove away from the main entrance gate, the blocks of Buchenwald became smaller and smaller. The crematorium chimney became shorter and shorter. And then they all disappeared, forever. Were they ever even there? Had I been there myself, I would not be sure.

The ride took almost five hours before the truck dropped us off at the train station in Pilsen. Accompanied by a local police escort, we were placed on a freight train waiting at the station. There were no seats, but we had plenty of room on the floor of the cars. All the Slovakian prisoners were still wearing their striped uniforms, but no one really minded. The smell of freedom was intoxicating. We were going back home to Slovakia.

When the train arrived in Bratislava, we were greeted at the station by members of the Joint and representatives of other Jewish organizations. We were given a warm meal, new clothes, and shoes.

They then sat us down in front of detailed survivor lists, but I couldn't find any of our family members' names there.

"What now?" asked Father.

"Let's keep calm. The fact that their names are not there doesn't mean anything. I think we should first seek Lizi and Erno," I answered. "If anyone managed to escape being captured, it would be Lizi."

My aunt and her husband had the best hiding arrangement of all. Uncle Erno Gallan was a bank clerk. He and my mother's sister Lizi lived on 41 Palisády Street in Bratislava during the war years. That apartment belonged to a non-Jewish friend of Lizi, a high-ranking official who let them stay there in the last few years.

We had no local currency to pay for a taxi, so we walked. I wanted to save the dollars.

"We should be ready to hear bad news or no news about Mother. Most of the captured Jews didn't make it back," I calmly said.

"She survived. She is the strongest person I know. If we made it out alive, she did as well."

He really believed that. I couldn't accept it because I'd spent long

141

months mourning my mother. I couldn't lower my guards now when we were so close to finding out her fate.

Lizi's apartment was on the third floor of the building. Exhausted by the journey, Father sat down to rest on the pavement while I climbed up and stood in front of the front door. The name 'Gallan' was printed on a simple wooden sign.

I took a long breath and rang the doorbell.

Noise and commotion inside.

The door opened, and loud, hysterical screaming ensued.

My grandmother, my aunts Lizi and Gisella, Uncle Erno, and seven-year-old Peter, Lizi's son, showered me with kisses. We cried and laughed and hugged and then cried again. Then they all stopped.

"Where is Zoli?" asked Grandmother.

"He is downstairs. He is weak," I said.

The shouts resumed but I took a step back.

"Where is she?" I asked.

"She is sleeping in the other room. She made it back a week ahead of you, and I'm sure that your story is as horrible as hers," said Aunt Lizi. "After we wash and feed you, we want to hear all about it."

Erno went down with me to help Father climb the stairs. Lizi and Gisella went to wake Mother and fixed everyone tea. Erno went out to call the doctor to come and check on us.

Both of us went in to see her in bed. She was as thin as Father and moved very slowly. I looked like a fat, privileged person, standing next to two breathing corpses. No words were said. There was not a lot of touching either, because Mother was washed and cleaned up, while Father and I smelled like garbage dumpsters and had months-old dirt and disease all over our bodies.

Father just put his finger on her forehead. "Hello Irena. We missed you so. We are going to wash up and eat something."

I don't think he had prepared for the reunion that morning or rehearsed any lines. It sounded like a reasonable thing to say.

She went back to sleep. Father fell asleep on the floor in the living room. He was too exhausted. I took the longest and most thorough bath of my young life. It took a hard brush and a full bar of soap to complete a proper cleansing. When Father woke up, I took him to the bath and helped him clean up. I couldn't recognize him afterwards. He no longer smelled like the stenchy *Muselmann* who had traveled with me from camp.

Our small family was reunited, and now also disinfected.

We spent a few days together in the apartment and, slowly and carefully, started sharing some of the painful events and experiences of the previous months.

Mother's story was unsurprisingly similar to ours. Typical of her, she told it with little emotion.

After we got separated at the train station in Nováky, she was transferred on a cattle train to Ravensbrück in northern Germany. Ravensbrück was the largest women's concentration camp in the Third Reich, and it housed both Jews and non-Jews. All these long months, she was being held about 300 kilometers away from us. She was detained with women from across Europe, including German, French, Russian, Greek, Italian, Belgian, Dutch, Polish, and Czech. She spoke of brave friendships with fellow inmates that helped her through her time there. While in the camp, she was forced to work at the Siemens armament factory, located an hour's walk from the camp. Like her husband, she alternated weekly between 12-hour day and night shifts. In the factory, she was initially part of the assembly line producing a highly detailed part of the V-1 Flying Bomb, which made the life of citizens in Southern England a living hell in 1944. She was then transferred to a depot where they loaded trains with cannon shells. Some days she was fed, others she was not. She referred to the cooked root vegetables they were served as cow food. Many thousands of the laborers in the camp died from malnutrition, disease, and Nazi brutality. On April 30, 1945, almost three weeks after the American units freed us in Buchenwald, her camp guards led a line of hundreds of the surviving prisoners to a nearby small town, left them there, and fled. Red Army units appeared minutes later. In total, she spent six months as a forced laborer in

Ravensbrück, not knowing anything about our fate and expecting the worst. After the Russians set her free, she experienced terrible ordeals making her way back to Bratislava, by horse cart, train, car, and foot. Arriving in the city, she spent time with a local Jewish organization, seeking information about her family. She found Ernest Gallan's name as a local bank employee and found her way to Erno's and Lizi's apartment. Lizi recalled that Mother looked like a walking skeleton when she first arrived at their door. They took her in, washed her thoroughly, and provided her with new clothes. She then went to bed and slept for days and days. They were careful to feed her in small doses, every few hours, until she regained her strength.

The large apartment had no electricity, only gas. Many survivors from our region found their way there in the coming weeks. Some stayed with us for hours, some for days. Grandmother cooked around the clock to feed everyone. We heard more brave survival stories about tragic suffering, hope, and despair.

Our family members, who used to live in our hometown and adjacent towns and villages, were mostly unaccounted for, presumed dead in the gas chambers of the Polish death camps. We knew that most of them were included in the mass transports of 1942 to destinations such as Auschwitz, Treblinka, Sobibor, and Majdanek. Among those we already knew had lost their lives were three of Father's sisters: Sara Friedman, with her husband and son, Margit Ornstein and her husband, Bronca and her husband, as well as Mother's brother Emerich and his wife, and dozens of cousins, second cousins, nephews, and nieces. For the most part, they were murdered by gas. The surviving leadership of the Slovakian Jewish community estimated that at least 50,000 local Jews had been killed in the death camps and elsewhere.

Among the stories, we heard that the Jewish informer Dov Schwartz, who had turned in our family the previous year, had run out of luck. The Gestapo trade kept him alive during the war, but his notoriety preceded him. Once the Germans skipped town, he was captured and hanged by the partisans in a nearby forest. Even good news tended to be rather morbid during that time.

I started having bad thoughts, consumed by guilt and survivor's remorse. A reoccurring dream of myself, standing on our rooftop in Sečovce, staring at a never-ending line of Jewish friends, neighbors, and fellow townsmen, walking towards the train station, and being led to their deaths, haunted my nights.

"Why are we alive and they are all dead, Father?"

"I don't know, Sanyi. I guess it's the luck of the draw. No rhyme or reason to it."

"Do you honestly think so? I admit that luck played a role, but we were also saved because you built a profitable business, and consequently strong relationships with non-Jews in our town, and they protected us through the worst of the deportation era."

"I disagree. Consider my poor sister Margit and her husband Nathan. They had a huge paint business, much bigger than ours, in Košice, before the war. They were wealthy, much richer than we ever were, and also very well connected, definitely at echelons much higher than us. It didn't save them."

"It can't all be luck."

"Well, the fact that we are back alive is not all because of luck. We fought to survive. We sincerely wanted to live. Luck gave us opportunities to fight, and that was a privilege most of our family members didn't have, unfortunately."

"Are we going to keep our false Ružiak name, or should we reissue papers under our real names?"

"I had given it some thought. Well, the name Rosenberg didn't bring us, or any other member of our family, much luck or value. The other name kept us alive. I vote that we stick with Ružiak."

We did.

One morning, a smiling Gisella came over and handed me the metal statue of the two French bulldogs.

"Every time we had bad thoughts, Mother and I used to pick up the dogs, and they made us believe we would see you again," she said. "How did you know to leave them with me before you were caught?"

"I just had this weird feeling that you should have them. It is now safe for them to come back home with me. Thank you for guarding them."

I placed the statue of the dogs over my bed.

We spent a few weeks with my aunts and Grandmother. My parents were almost fully recovered physically.

"We should travel back to Košice. I want to see my friends and visit our home," I said over breakfast.

"Sanyi, we discussed it and I'm not sure it's a good idea. Our home is gone. Our family is not there anymore. You should consider this more carefully."

After being fully independent at Gustloff and Buchenwald, it was challenging for me to step back into the role of a 17-year-old in the custody of his hands-on, micromanaging parents.

"You don't have to join me. I'll go there myself."

"You will not. If you insist and want to go there so badly, I will try again to convince Mother to agree that we head out together."

I insisted. And they succumbed and agreed to join me.

And then Uncle Bella returned from the war to see us in Bratislava.

Growing up in Trebišov, Uncle Bella Rosenbaum had been a born socialist with a natural passion for justice and equality, and outright contempt towards organized religion and Anglo-Saxon capitalism. In his childhood, he was educated in the *Hashomer Hatzair* youth movement in Trebišov, where he developed a strong solidarity with Russian communism. This is where he met his girlfriend Ilonka, who shared his world views. When the war started, a non-Jewish friend in Trebišov provided Bella with false documents under the name Michal Kazimir. Before joining the fight against the Nazis, he traveled with Ilonka to Bratislava, and arranged for her to stay in the safe house apartment with his mother and young sister Gisella. That was the apartment we sought when we fled on the train from Michalovce. Bella then sought to help the Russian war effort by joining the Slovak partisans fighting the Germans in the Lower Tatri mountains. When the Red Army advanced into Slovakia and liberated the entire Tatri area, he volunteered and formally enlisted, unlike most Slovakian Jews. He fought shoulder-to-shoulder with his Russian comrades all the way to Berlin and was honorably discharged as a sergeant. A modest man, upon returning from Germany, he nevertheless drove back to Bratislava in an expensive, shiny convertible that once belonged to a high-ranking German general in the capital. The car was gifted to him by top Russian officials to acknowledge his devoted service. He was now walking the streets of Bratislava wearing a Russian army uniform, flat broke. His uniform granted him free gasoline for his sweet ride. He now permanently changed his name to Michal Kazimir, his wartime assumed identity.

I always loved his big heart and wittiness but couldn't really connect to his philosophical views.

We were so happy to see him again and listen to his war stories. One night he took me out to a small German restaurant and treated me to a suckling pig knuckle. It was divine.

"What are your future plans?" Bella asked me.

"I really don't know," I answered. "I've missed many years in school, so first and foremost I want to complete my education, and then I thought about joining my uncles in America. There's nothing left for us in Slovakia."

"Indeed, nothing left here. However, I would urge you to consider not emigrating to a capitalist, cruel place like America. You will become a slave to a business owner, underpaid and undertreated. I truly believe that the end of this war will expedite a proletariat-led revolution. We must take advantage of the carnage around us to better the situation of the regular folk, the working men and women."

"You always loved reading Marx and I'm sure you found like-minded friends in the Red Army." I laughed. "I don't intend to work for anyone but myself, whether in America, Czechoslovakia, or elsewhere. I am also not interested in these politics."

"These are not politics. It's about your, and your children's future. I believe that the Soviet Union has a better, albeit not perfect, model for living. A hundred years from today, communism will rule because people will become disenchanted with, and harmed by, greedy capitalism."

"We'll see. In the meantime, I intend to practice capitalism as a small-business owner in some country," I concluded.

Bella came back from the war accompanied by a Polish friend named Alex, who had fought alongside him. When Alex heard of our plan to travel back from Bratislava to Košice, he suggested that he join us. In those days, a train trip to Košice was complicated. Most of the railway bridges in Slovakia had been blown up during the war, and the only possible train route was a long detour through Budapest in Hungary. Moreover, trains did not arrive or depart according to any preset schedule after the war. There were no conductors, or any authorized personnel that kept order at the stations or on the trains. Whoever wanted, and was able to, boarded the trains.

"What a wonderful idea!" I said. Better to travel with a Red Army sergeant in uniform as your companion than without one.

We left eastbound a few days later.

Alex was wearing his neatly pressed uniform. He confidently led us through the station as we boarded a very crowded train and stepped ahead of us into a completely full car.

"Everybody out! Go to the next car immediately! That's an order!" he shouted. "This train car is for official use only."

It took five seconds for all passengers to clear the car. Alex shut the door behind us, not before he wrote and attached a note to the door, claiming that the particular train car was reserved for Russian officials traveling on formal state business. There were five passengers seated there now: my parents and myself, Alex, and a Jewish woman who had befriended Mother in Ravensbrück and had asked to join us. In the previous weeks she had also been staying with the Gallans, waiting for an opportunity to head back to Eastern Slovakia to look for her husband, children, and any other surviving family members.

A few hours into the trip, we stopped at a station in Hungary so the dispatcher could switch the tracks. We had to wait there for a few hours. As our train stood, another train that was heading east stopped on the adjacent track. It was a cattle train, and as we learned later, filled with German families, traveling with young children and all their belongings.

"Open the window, I want to climb down for a moment," Alex directed me.

I had no idea what he was up to.

"Catch the suitcases I'll be throwing your way momentarily." He winked and climbed down before I was able to protest. He was about to pillage the passengers in the other train.

"This is appalling," said Mother. "The man is a brute. Can't you stop him?" she was no longer the rough camp survivor; she was now back to being her old noble self.

"Not really. He's a big boy and won't listen to me," I answered.

We were passively participating in yet another act of wartime cruelty. I'd been witnessing so many of those in recent years. During the war, at times, humans lost their humanity.

I stood next to the window and followed Alex with my eyes. He entered one of the cars, shouted a few words, and started looking around. I could see terror in the eyes of the travelers, men, women, and children. He started weighing different suitcases with his hands. Once satisfied, Alex left the car with a number of items of luggage, crossed to the other tracks and started tossing the bags to me through the window.

"Who are you? What business do you have here stealing suitcases?"

Out of nowhere appeared the Russian officer in charge of the other train, after he saw Alex throwing the suitcases into our train.

"Hand me your papers. I don't care if you're a Russian soldier, this is a special government convoy. What do you think you are doing, you bloody thief?"

Standing in the gap between the trains, Alex became white as snow and handed over his papers. He was taken at gunpoint into the officers' car. We thought that was the last we had seen of him, as our train was just about to leave the station.

Just in time, he made it back and climbed up into the car, still pale and visibly shaken.

"Are you okay? What was that all about?" I asked.

"I was very close to being court-martialed for looting. Luckily, I'm usually good at talking my way out of trouble. My challenge is usually to keep out of it."

"But what happened?"

"The train across the tracks is a formal Russian Government dispatch train. It is hosting all the German engineers, physicists, and other professionals from the Zeiss factory in Jena, along with their families, as well as loads of technical equipment. Apparently, they are all sent to Russia to form a Soviet optics factory."

"Why would the families and scientists agree to do that?"

"Well, frankly, I don't think they were given a choice. German spoils are currently being divided up and handed over to the winning nations, and I guess the Soviet Union got to keep some optics assets now. I'm sure they will treat the families very kindly, because they need the cooperation of the scientists."

He did manage to toss in three suitcases before getting caught. He opened them and all they contained were articles of food. Alex explained that his selection criteria depended solely on weight. His assumption was that heavier items were more likely to contain gold and silver. Apparently not.

My parents were visibly disgusted by his acts.

I was tired of war, looting, hustling for canned food or a dried loaf of bread. It'd been many weeks since the Germans surrendered, but the old society order still eluded us. Acts of indecency and injustice, caused by the general lawlessness that prevailed all around, were abundant. We all craved order, but there was no way to know when to expect it, so we had to brace ourselves.

After a long voyage, we arrived in Košice, via Budapest. Alex bid us farewell and left. The three of us stayed with distant relatives as we couldn't afford paying for a hotel. Consequently, we could only spend a few days in town.

I was contemplating returning to visit Sečovce but was dissuaded by everyone I spoke to. They said that all the people we had known were not there anymore. My peers who had survived the war were now living in Košice, the regional capital. Because they couldn't attend school during the war, many of them were taking expedited courses to obtain their high school diplomas.

I spent some time with a good friend who was a year older than I was, Emerich (Emre) Klein, one of my only schoolmates who had made it back alive. Emre's parents owned a small cafe in the city, and he was one of the only people I knew who had received a formal affidavit that allowed him to legally travel to Palestine. During one of our meetings, he introduced me to a beautiful young woman, Judith Ackerman. I hung out at the café with Judith and Emre a couple of times and our interactions made it clearer to me that our family no longer belonged in our homeland of Eastern Slovakia. Everyone was making plans to go elsewhere and restart their lives.

Mother made sure that her old friends in Sečovce, Maria and Katarina, were made aware that she was back and staying in Košice, and she sent them a message that they were invited to come and pay her a visit. She couldn't stand the thought of going into either of their homes and seeing her neatly collected and curated furniture.

Maria and Katarina arrived at our relatives' apartment late one morning.

"Our dear Irena, I am so happy to see you alive! We were worried sick and couldn't find out anything about you. I cried tears of joy when I read your letter." Maria rushed to hug Mother.

Mother's eyes were cold. She didn't utter a word.

"We were so concerned when you just disappeared, we thought we would never see you again." Katarina put her hand on Mother's shoulder.

Mother, who was not known for her warmth, was as frozen as

Antarctica in peak winter. "Let's sit down in the living room, I don't want to speak in front of Alexander."

The three of them left us and shut the foyer door behind them.

I put my ear on the door.

"Thank you for coming to see me. I am tired and still not well, so you will excuse me if our meeting this morning will not last too long."

"Of course, Irena. How are you doing? Are you in pain? Where do you live now? How are Zoli and Alexander?" They both interjected with questions.

"We are fine, thank you for asking."

There was a long silence before Mother spoke again. "My family went through hell in the last three years. We were hunted down, captured, tortured, forced to work for the Nazis, deprived of sleep, food, and water, treated like dogs, and yet we survived against all odds. Everything was taken away from us. They took our names, our home, our business, our belongings, our furniture, our dignity. I lost my clothes and my jewelry. We will never recover from this." Her laconic voice gave away no emotion. I could imagine her eyes staring at the wall, not looking at the women sitting in front of her.

Another long pause. Then she continued. "I always thought of you as our friends, as my friends-"

"But we are your friends, Irena," Maria cut her off, her voice breaking.

Long pause.

"I thought you were my friends," she repeated and continued in a stagnant voice. "You went to great efforts to appropriate my property, furs, and furniture. Neither of you thought of me as a human being, whose life mattered, whose life was worth saving."

At that point I started hearing the two guests sobbing.

"I am so sorry for everything you went through, so sorry," a crying Katarina mumbled. "What could we have done? They would have killed us too if we had resisted. Also, the Russians took away all of your precious belongings when they occupied our town. Like you, we lost everything!"

"I admired you both. You were so intelligent and nice and educated and beautiful and fashionable. All that time, you despised us. And when you had a chance, you turned your backs on us, after making off with my carpets and chandeliers. You are bad people, and your conscience will carry the burden of your deeds until the day you die. I never want to see you again. Please leave here at once," said Mother in conclusion.

The door opened and she went out, continued to the corridor and into her room, slamming the door behind her. Maria and Katarina walked out of the room after her, their eyes red, holding onto decorated handkerchiefs and blank expressions, and left. Mother never saw them again.

We returned to Bratislava the next day.

11 CASERTA

I was now an 18-year-old World War II veteran, whose past, identity, and childhood had been all but taken away and wiped out. I had to dig deep inside to decide who I was, and what my new life should be like. Czechoslovakia was no longer my country, and my hometown was no longer my home. My country turned against me, made me its enemy, persecuted me, and tried to assassinate me, and didn't even care to issue an apology or any compensation. For all our past generations and everything we managed to build, did we ever belong here at all? At night, I was dreaming about concentration camp roll calls, watery soups, picking winter weed roots and leafy veggies with French prisoners and being locked long hours in windowless train cars, surrounded by dead bodies. During the day, I couldn't find my place.

Do I return to school? Should I immigrate to the newly founded state of Israel, like some other young Jewish survivors, who saw their calling in defending the Jewish State? Do I board a ship to America and try my luck there? Who will take care of my parents if I leave? I couldn't leave just yet.

My capable, technically skilled hands saved our family and

myself multiple times during our plight in recent years. Knowing that my passion and interest lay in the world of analog mechanics, I decided against going back to regular high school. Instead, I applied to a technical school that issued diplomas to adult career changers. Obviously, I was the youngest person in class.

With the kind help of Uncle Bella, who pulled a few bureaucratic strings, my parents managed to receive a government-sponsored two-room apartment in Bratislava. The apartment was owned by a German family that did not return after the war, and was already equipped with dishes, silverware, and furniture. There were also plenty of clothes in the closets.

Once again, Father couldn't find himself professionally in Bratislava. There were few available retail positions, and he couldn't land any of them. His luck changed when he received a letter from one of his surviving nephews, Alexander (Pitiu) Ornstein. Pitiu was the only son of Father's sister Margit, who had married Nathan Ornstein and moved from Sečovce to Košice months before I was born. Before the war, they owned and operated a large and successful wholesale paint business in Košice. The business included a spacious flagship store that had a huge basement with thousands of paint powder barrels. Their business was the largest residential paint operation in Eastern Slovakia. Both Margit and Nathan were murdered in Treblinka. Pitiu survived and had just gotten married in Budapest. In his letter, he asked Father to move back east and take over managing his late parents' paint store. Father was thrilled.

And so, just a few months after my school year began, my parents decided to move back to Košice so Father could take over the murdered Ornstein's business. I liked the idea of staying alone in Bratislava and learned to cook for myself, got to know the city well, and visited my old grandmother very often. My freedom and happiness were hampered by the emotional letters arriving from my parents, separately, begging me to join them. Recent war memories weighing heavily on my conscience, I decided to relocate back to Košice and start my second school year there. On the positive side, I couldn't forget the good times Judith and I had spent together during my last trip, and I was eager to see her again.

My heart didn't lie.

Seeing Judith again, I knew that the decision to return to Košice was the right one. She was bright and positive, beaming with joy of life, and I much needed to surround myself with optimism. Judith was born in my hometown. Her grandfather from her mother's side was a melamed [Jewish teacher], and that side of the family was very poor. They later moved to Uzhhorod, across the Ukrainian border, about an hour's drive from Sečovce. Father knew her mother, Lilly Adler, and her uncles Hershu and Shamu. Simon Ackerman, her father, had served in the Austro-Hungarian army and fought on the Albanian front during World War I. He was originally from the small village of Svetus, located between Uzhhorod and Sečovce, on the Slovakian side of the border. Svetus and its surrounding lands used to belong to Simon's father before the war. Under Nazi occupation, Simon, Lily, Judith, and her young sister Eva hid for months in a pigsty in the backyard of their house that had become their servants' home. Eva did not survive, but Judith and her parents did. Judith told me all these stories, and I understood that her positivity was a facade, covering unbearable pain and survivor guilt, for being *the sister that lived*. We were all traumatized, trying to handle reality under the clouds of unspeakable losses and tragic lives. During the war, she became an avid Zionist, strongly advocating that Jews should make their way back to their homeland of Palestine and form a Jewish state.

Father worked at the Ornstein paint store for a few months until he managed to stabilize operations and hire a permanent manager. With the money he earned, he started his own small grocery store. A few months later, he was asked by a competitor to take over and manage a much larger store, which he did, leaving Mother to handle the smaller location. Relatively quickly, they sold their small store to the competitor, and they both became salaried employees.

Judith and I started spending more time together in public. We took long walks in the center of town, frequented a local café where our friends would meet us, and hiked around the lakes down south.

Mother said we were a beautiful couple. People mistook us for being a brother and sister, because, well, we looked very similar.

"Are you planning to propose to Judith?" asked Mother during dinner.

I was caught off guard. "Why are you asking?"

"Well, she won't wait forever. You've been seeing each other for a few months now, and you need to decide. You are almost 21."

"I don't think I'm ready to talk about this."

"Suit yourself. I just wanted to share my thoughts."

Marriage was an idea that had not crossed my mind.

Upon graduation from school, I decided to continue my studies and pursue a diploma in mechanical engineering. There was only one institution offering this curriculum, located in nearby Prešov. I was admitted by mail, and by mid-September 1948 I was already preparing to leave for Prešov in preparation for the coming school year.

My mechanical talents had saved us from certain death at Buchenwald. There was no better omen for me. Arriving at my new school, I had time to reflect on how my future as a free man might look. The thought of going to America obsessed me. My talents, discipline, and entrepreneurial genes fit well with an untapped, vast market of opportunity. Daydreaming, I saw myself sitting in a small typewriter workshop in New York or Cleveland or Los Angeles, then opening another store location, and then another, then leasing a hangar full of typewriters, with trucks dropping off and picking up crates of product. How was life for Alexander, Simon, and Lawrence Rosenberg since crossing the Atlantic? For one, they were saved from the horrors of war. Judith would love it there, I knew. America!

Just as I was settling down in Prešov and blueprinting my North American conquests, I received a letter from Judith. She announced her decision to immigrate to the newly born State of Israel, in the midst of its War of Independence, and asked me to join her. Another war was not my plan, as I just managed to escape the last one by the skin of my teeth. Would she at least consider America?

It was decision time. Or maybe a decision had already been made for me. There was no choice but to find out.

By the next day, I was sitting in front of Judith in Košice. I was rehearsing my America pitch over and over during the train ride. Alas, that pitch didn't turn out that well. Judith had the power of destiny and historical deliverance on her side. She was also very persuasive and charming.

"Are you sure about this?" I asked, after a long, lopsided dialogue.

"I am. And I want you to join me on this journey. I've got it all planned. We'll get married this week in town hall and attend military training to prepare us for the war."

"Wait, what military training?"

Judith smiled. "There is war in Palestine, and we have to help our brothers and sisters there. Next Monday, they are kicking off a volunteer training course in a small village called Sterlna, near Olomouc. I have registered us both."

"So, I guess you won't consider getting married and going to, for example, Cleveland, Ohio, in America?"

Judith continued smiling and shook her head from left to right.

We got married two days later in Košice, with both pairs of parents present.

For the following three months, we were trained by the Czechoslovakian army on behalf of the *Haganah*, the Jewish paramilitary organization that later became the IDF, the Israeli Defense Forces. The small town was emptied of its inhabitants and was solely used for training purposes. I trained as a Russian T-34 tank team member, specializing in artillery. Judith was being trained as a member of an anti-aircraft unit, filling the role of the person measuring distances to aerial targets. She had a meter-long telescope, which she used in order to identify the model of the plane and to estimate the altitude of enemy planes based on their profile. She would then transmit the data over radio frequency to the anti-aircraft artillery unit. She spent days studying all types of aircraft. We also received basic military training, including operating grenades and small firearms.

In December of 1948, Judith and I said our goodbyes in Košice. Our parents agreed to join us in Israel once the war was over and we were settled in.

"Mother, please take care of him. I brought him back to you safely from Germany, make sure you join us when you can."

"I promise, Sanyi. Be careful. Once we get our affairs in order here, and the war ends, you will see me there, in the desert. Who would have thought?"

"Here," I said as I handed her the statue of the French bulldogs. "Safeguard them for me until we reunite. When you get on the ship to Israel, please don't forget to bring them back to me."

She accepted them and smiled.

Judith and I took a train to Italy and boarded the Jewish refugee ship Caserta, making its way to the old Israeli port of Jaffa. We didn't have a dime in our pockets, didn't speak the local language, were terrified of the war with all the surrounding Arab armies, and were not at all ready for the Middle Eastern heat. But we were excited to reinvent ourselves purposefully and to find ourselves a new home. Our old one didn't exist anymore.

The Caserta was not a luxury vessel, but everyone on board was pumped up with adrenaline and less concerned with the quality of food, lodging, or hygiene.

I was strolling on the upper deck and started a conversation with a tall man who seemed to be about my age. He introduced himself as Samuel, a labor camp survivor and volunteer from the Netherlands. We were shading our eyes from the sun and staring at the calm Mediterranean waters.

"Our lifelong dream is about to come true," said Samuel, unable to hide his emotions. "I want to fight for our country."

It still sounded funny to me, hearing everyone speak about "their country" when referring to a place they had never visited.

"The situation there is so complicated," he continued. "The British supreme command folded its flag in May, shipped its last remaining officers and staff to London, and that same night, Prime Minister Ben Gurion declared the establishment of the State of Israel. The next day, all neighboring, and some non-neighboring, Arab armies invaded our land, and the war has been raging ever since, with our forces being outnumbered at least by a ratio of ten-to-one. Our whole country has a population of 600,000, mostly comprised of Jewish immigrants from Europe who survived the Nazis, and they are fighting trained troops from Egypt, Syria, Lebanon, Jordan, Iraq, as well as Palestinian militias."

"Sounds like a dire situation for us," I answered, even though nothing in his overview was new to me.

"There were a number of declared truces, but none held for very long. The third and last one was announced just a couple of months ago. There is now fierce fighting going on in the north, on the Lebanese border, and down south with the Egyptians."

"I know. We were briefed at the camp in Slovakia before we left for Italy. I am sure that our spirit and solidarity will help our army prevail and force an armistice soon. The one thing that concerned me was weaponry. Do you think such a small army will be able to continue fighting the war using old British and French guns and equipment?" I asked.

"I agree. Our spirit shall prevail," he answered. "And regarding weaponry, we heard at our farewell briefing that the Allies are arranging to send boatloads of captured German guns to support our army. Imagine all those tens of thousands of Mauser rifles. That will surely tilt the balance of power in the battlefield."

A chilling thought went through my mind. Somewhere, on this earth or in the heavens, Grischa was now laughing at the karma of a sabotaged Mauser operated on the battlefield by Alexander, the original saboteur. Oh my, it was about to get really interesting...

The port of Jaffa revealed itself through the light morning clouds.

We were the group of "volunteers" from Czechoslovakia referred to as the "Czech Brigade." We were 1,500 men and women, all camp survivors. The Caserta carried approximately 500 of us. After the ship docked, we disembarked on a dreary day and were immediately sent to our military units. Judith and I were assigned to different battalions. Our first challenge was to find ways to communicate so we could find each other. We agreed to write letters every week to the liaison office in Tel Aviv and hoped for the best.

A platoon consisting of 100 new recruits from the Czech Brigade, including myself, was initially stationed in Beit Lid, a ruined and deserted Arab village. It was a huge transfer center located in a base vacated by Her Majesty's Army when it hastily left Palestine the previous year, about 30 kilometers north of Tel Aviv. The army wisely kept large groups from the same country of origin together, so their members could communicate effectively. How do you run an army, fighting for the life of a nascent country, when most soldiers don't speak the local language?

The compound consisted of some old buildings and many tents, housing new immigrants from around the world. They rounded us up upon arrival in the afternoon, gave us uniforms, and sent us to sleep. A young sergeant came in the morning, and shouted orders to head out and form a lineup. Just like magic, 100 Czechs and Slovaks, trained overseas to understand basic Hebrew military terms and orders, formed a perfect lineup. The others, from Morocco, Libya, Romania, and other places, were completely lost. Surprised, the sergeant started ordering us to march to the right and to the left, and our brigade performed immaculately, singing Hebrew marching hymns. He couldn't believe it and ran to bring out the officers to experience this wonder. They were all fascinated, and immediately asked us to march through the entire camp, to give the example of how the Jewish army could look if soldiers were disciplined. Two days later, we were ordered to conduct a parade in the nearby coastal city of Netanya, near the Esther Cinema, on the cliffs overlooking the Mediterranean, hosted by *Hava'ad Le-Ma'an Hachayal,* a volunteer body that took care of the immigrant soldiers. We marched all the way from Beit Lid to Esther Cinema. Thousands of Netanya residents came out to witness the new, emerging Israeli army marching on. It came to the attention of Prime Minister Ben Gurion that the Czech Brigade had strong military skills and discipline. Rumor had it that upon hearing the report, the Old Man popped a fuse, called the secretary of defense, and warned him that the young state was experiencing "an organized communist infiltration that must be dissolved at once." A few days later, we were all separated into various army units around the country.

Other than understanding basic orders, I couldn't speak any Hebrew when I was met by the army representative in the port of Jaffa. There was no way for me to communicate the fact that I was a weapons expert, nor did I know if there were any Czech or German weapons already in use by the Israeli army.

"Ich bin ein Waffen Meister!" I exclaimed in German to the officer in the Beit Lid camp.

He looked at me, nodded, and shipped me off to an infantry battalion. Initially, I was stationed in a unit in charge of guarding prisoners of war, mostly Egyptians, in Tel Hashomer base. The camp was surrounded with barbed wire, and we patrolled the external yard with rifles, in 12-hour shifts, which felt familiar from another camp I used to live in. After a short period, I was transferred to a battalion in Be'er Ya'acov.

Every few weeks, I was allowed to spend a weekend away from my unit.

From the ship in Jaffa, Judith was transferred to and stationed in Zrifin camp. Our only local contact was a cousin of mine named Alex Brown, who lived and worked in a small fish processing company in Tel Aviv's Montefiore neighborhood. Judith and I both knew his home address. Whenever one of us got time off, that person would head to Brown's place, assess the situation, and then go back and report about the other's spouse. On the weekends when we were both back, we needed to find a place to get some privacy. Hotel Savoy, at the time a decrepit, small building on Hayarkon Street, had a

Hungarian owner, whom we got to know. Feeling sorry for the newlyweds, he offered us a small kitchenette that we could use.

As a married woman, Judith was discharged from the army after three months. She had no place to go as we were flat broke. When she left the army, she and a friend got a bed in a large communal room from the city officer of Tel Aviv.

My new commanding officer was a Hungarian speaker from Kibbutz Dgania. I mentioned to him time and again that I was a weapons expert, but he didn't act on it. I persisted, because I felt my skills and expertise were being wasted. Peeking into our unit's armory shed, all I could see was one big mess. There were landmines and bullets tossed everywhere, dirt and rubbish, and no order whatsoever. By that time, I'd built up a high level of frustration, and was able to speak some useful Hebrew. I now understood Israeli mentality and had a plan. Nice guys don't get anywhere in the Land of Milk and Honey.

One evening, the battalion was preparing a night reconnaissance patrol, from Be'er Ya'acov to the sea and back. Pretending to be injured, I asked not to join the unit. My commander made me leave with the unit anyway. At some point during the night, around the sand dunes of Rishon Le'Zion, I stopped and said I could go no further. They left me alone there. Two men were sent back to look for me, and I refused to continue with them. The unit picked me up on their way back. The next day, my officer, who understood he could no longer disregard my pleas, came to visit and asked what it was that I wanted to do. I repeated my story about Gustloff and my deep knowledge in light weaponry. I explained to him that the unit did not have any weapons experts, and that I could bring them a lot of benefits. He begrudgingly agreed.

I was sent to the armory the next day, without a designated role. In the tent, I met two soldiers, the Polish sergeant Svirsky and a private who kept his mouth shut. Once I picked up a Czech rifle and started dismantling it, they both understood I knew what I was doing. They allowed me to go ahead and tidy up the armory. Over the course of 14 straight hours, I took out everything to the yard, then used a broom, washed the room, fixed the rifle stand, cleaned, and oiled each and every one of the rifles, and then separated the landmines, detonators, and bullets. When the sergeant came back the next morning, he could hardly believe his eyes. I then went to invite the Hungarian officer to look at the armory. He came to me and shook my hand.

For the next year and a half, the remainder of my service, I functioned as a weapons expert. Towards the end of the war, I was transferred to the Ninth Battalion of the Negev Brigade, which was responsible for the entire southern front. The battalion was based in Julis, which seemed like the end of the world. The armory I was responsible for supplied ammunition and firearms to all the units and posts in the region, all the way down to Eilat, Israel's southernmost point. I would go on ten-day command car trips at a time, followed by two ammunition trucks, driving between all southern bases, from point to point. None of the roads was paved; it was all dust and soil. We were always dirty as hell. The area was known as Fedayeen Country, and we feared vicious terrorist attacks at night.

Coming back from one of those tours of duty, Judith and I sat on the beach in Tel Aviv to watch another beautiful sunset.

"Do you think our lives will ever be normal? Will we be able to escape the cycle of war and death?" I asked. "I'm starting to think that we are the ones who bring this suffering wherever we go."

"Stop your nonsense and take a look around," she replied with her laughing eyes. "This is your land, our land, your yet-to-be-born children's land. One day, you will be sitting with your grandson and telling him the sad and happy stories of how, against all odds, his family made it."

I hoped she was right. As a 22-year-old veteran of two historical wars, I'd had enough adventure to last me a lifetime.

PART 2
OREN

12 MAJDANEK

1992, NETANYA, ISRAEL

They used to call them *The Polish Pilgrims* in the 1990s. These high
school group trips to the Nazi death camps in Poland had become a
rite of passage for Israeli youth, as well as a powerful state tool to
embolden young souls, just before they embarked on a multiyear,
obligatory military service, to volunteer for the most dangerous
combat units. The defense ministry and army would send officials to
meet the groups and speak in front of highly emotional young
audiences at the entrance gates to Auschwitz-Birkenau, the most
notorious of the Nazi death camps. They explained that Jews were
no longer led to slaughter, because soldiers-to-be like us would
defend their families and country. At 17, I regarded that state act as
the most despicable, cynical, psychological abuse. I still think so
today, although with a better understanding of the motives behind
this policy. Nevertheless, I went on a *Polish Pilgrimage* in 1992,
because I wanted to date a girl.

Please don't get me wrong. As a teenager, I respected my people's
tragic past immensely. I respected my grandfather's survival journey
more than anything else in the world.

We were a family of survivors that lost many of its members

during the Holocaust. My grandfather and his late parents hid during the war, they were then captured and taken to concentration camps Buchenwald and Ravensbrück before being liberated by the Americans and Russians in 1945. Grandfather survived intact, more or less. He suffered from chronic stomach issues as a result of a brutal beating by a German officer while at the concentration camp. He spent years seeking expert opinions about this physical injury from the war.

I lost my father, an air force combat pilot, when I was a baby, when his jet collided midair with another friendly fighter plane. Grandfather Alex stepped in and became my father figure. Since I was three, he repeatedly told me his childhood and adolescence stories, with all tales of horror, omitting no detail. I just never could stand the thought of my government profiting politically from humanity's darkest hour, from the travails of its tortured citizens, my family.

"Oren! are you joining the 11th-grade trip to Poland this year?" asked Michelle as we were walking out of the chemistry lab. "I can't wait. The thought of going there excites me and at the same time totally freaks me out. I just feel like I have to go."

"Not sure," I replied. "I have to think about it. Maybe I'll speak to my grandpa about it."

"How is Alexander doing?" she asked. "He's the coolest grandad ever. Last time I saw him was when he did his famous magic show at your birthday party. How's his health?"

"He's getting old in style, but he's stronger than us all. Still running his office automation business empire in full force, globetrotting like crazy."

"Is he still passionately proclaiming his life mantras?" she giggled.

"Hell yeah!" I smiled back and signaled with three of my fingers. "*Positive thinking, life is good,* and the quintessential *if I don't take care of myself, no one else will take care of me.*"

I was on the fence about joining the trip and couldn't make up my mind. A couple of good friends of mine, Michelle included, announced they were signing up.

Somewhere deep I always felt as if the souls of my family members had been residing there, hovering over the death and concentration camps, never really leaving the blood-soaked valleys and the damned crematoriums of Europe after the war. I didn't actually feel the need to physically return there, because we had never actually left.

"Why would you want to go to the Nazi camps in Poland?" My concerned grandfather furrowed his brows. "I thought I had taught you better. You know the past well. I told you all our stories. Many of the Poles were accomplices. They were very bad people. My aunts' and uncles' blood is on their hands. Let's live our lives and focus on the here and now." He then offered that we both fly back to his favorite casino in Baden-Baden, suggesting that a German all-inclusive holiday resort had much more to offer me than a Polish death camp museum. He knew me too well. Our grandfather-grandson excursions to Germany had become legendary. I took pleasure in seeing him walking around, living, and breathing, in Germany. He was a different man. Like a fish put back in water, so was Alexander Ružiak around the German language and culture. Plus, he exuded such delight from being alive and pampered by German waiters and concierges, on German soil, be it in a hotel, spa, restaurant, or casino.

"That's exactly what came to my mind, Grandpa. I will let them know I won't be joining. Let's look at dates for our trip!"

Michelle was disappointed when I told her.

"Oh no... please, please reconsider. This is the one opportunity when you get to visit all of these horrendous sites, with me! And other friends as well, obviously. You know so much of the history through your family stories, you can share that with all of us there. Would you at least make it to the pre-trip prep meeting today? There are other guys who are undecided about the trip who'll be there. If you still decide not to join, following the meeting, I'll let it go."

I told her I would make it to the meeting, but made sure she didn't build any expectations.

The get-together took place at the school gym right after dismissal. I walked in and grabbed an empty back-row seat next to another classmate who was sincerely debating whether to go on the trip. I apologized in advance and told him I'd probably leave after a few minutes.

Other students came in and filled the room.

"Who's that?" My senses perked up.

She was sitting next to Michelle, on the other side of the room. In one hand, she was holding the book *Night* by Elie Wiesel, the world's most famous Holocaust survivor. Her other hand was flipping through a pamphlet titled, "Poland Trip 1992: What You Absolutely Need to Know." She was reading it intently.

"New girl," my classmate said. "Her name is Hannah. Her family moved from Haifa. Don't know her. Michelle has been hanging out with her."

Hannah was studiously following our history teacher, Ms. Stein, as she made her presentation about the trip, and asked a question that caused the teacher to lose her rhythm. She inquired whether the trip leadership would agree to structure the journey as more of an individual learning experience process, rather than engineering the schedule as a fully scripted, pre-planned, state-formal affair. The teacher muttered a long reply about how the school was tied to the national Holocaust learning program that limited their flexibility. A dialogue ensued between the two. Undoubtedly ahead of her years, Hannah wasn't there to appease. She was beautiful and articulate, and I wanted to spend more time with, and get to know Hannah.

"Wait, didn't you say you were leaving?"

"I decided to stay," I told my friend. "Really fascinating discussion."

"It is our duty to go to the Nazi camps in Poland," said Ms. Stein. "Most of the Poles were innocent victims of the occupation and German cruelty, like Jews, Gypsies, and gay people. Only when you experience the land, the towns, the people, the surrounding villages, the smells, nature, and the food, will you be able to immerse yourself in our tragic history."

My hand raised itself. "Wanted to reiterate Hannah's point," I heard myself speak decisively in front of the room. "Hearing the stories of students and visitors coming back from the camps, their experiences were personal and varying. To me, this visit is more a spiritual and emotional experience than a fact-finding mission. It's important you allow us the space to experience, rather than be led by a stringent agenda."

Hannah noticed me for the first time.

I naturally didn't look back at her. My heartbeat rate was soaring.

I called Michelle after the session and told her that If Hannah wasn't dating anyone and decided to go to Poland, I would definitely be in. I could see her grinning through the curled, analogue phone line. The next morning, she confirmed Hannah was both available and committed to the trip. I updated my grandfather about my decision to go, not sharing my motives. I'm sure he would have definitely approved had I told him about Hannah.

Cursed motherland, I am coming back to you!

We were a group of 25 students and three teacher-chaperones. The flight to Warsaw left Ben Gurion Airport a few weeks later. It was winter.

It took three days, a walking tour of Krakow, and our first extermination camp visit to make Hannah and me inseparable. We laughed and talked for hours at night, until her roommate kicked me out. We made out in the hotel, in the back of the bus when everyone was out to lunch, and behind the tourist center at Treblinka. We were shameless. We fell deeply in love during a week everyone expected us to be deeply in pain and grief. We talked about how emotionally detached we were of the savagery surrounding us, stories, and exhibits, and tried to make sense of it. And then we would make out again.

The teachers didn't care much for our public displays of

affection, and separately called out Hannah and me to convey their disappointment in our insensitive behavior.

"Is this some kind of a teenage psychological defense mechanism?" asked Ms. Zimmerman, one of the teachers accompanying the group. "I expect more from both of you!"

I always suspected that none of these old, grumpy teachers had ever proper teenage experiences themselves. Now I had the undeniable proof.

She continued. "I know this trip could be very traumatic. I understand that some of you may seek a shoulder to cry on, but... could you please dial it down a notch, young man? I want you to feel this wretched place deeply. I want you to connect with our history."

I didn't "feel" the place or the connection and didn't really expect to. Listening to tragic family tales from the war since early childhood, I rarely became emotional over anything. A school trip wasn't about to change that.

Hannah and I talked about our teacher chats later that evening.

"Do you think this means we are bad people?" she asked, and all I wanted to do was kiss her lips again.

"I truly think my great-great uncles and aunts who perished in these camps would highly approve of us enjoying the here and now that Poland has to offer because life is fragile and short," I said, while maneuvering under her blouse. "They would have done the same."

"Stop, let's be serious. I want to talk about this for a minute," she said, and I pulled back. "Maybe the teachers are right. Maybe because all we can see is each other right now, we don't really allow ourselves the space to connect with the world around us, or with our emotions." She paused. "The purpose of this trip is too important to me, I've waited a long time to come here," she added in a whisper and stared at me with her big brown eyes.

"Wait, what are you saying?" My smirk vanished. I didn't like where this discussion was heading.

"Let's take a break," she gently put her hand on my face. "Let's disengage so we give each other a chance to truly immerse ourselves in this trip. I hope you take this the right way."

I knew she was right. Her unwavering style made her so amazing. A decision had been made for me, and there was nothing much I could do about it. I went back to my room, defeated.

I didn't really feel anything the next day as well, listening to more testimonies, visiting another camp, going through documents, sitting through team discussions. Was there something wrong with me? More importantly, did Hannah believe there was something wrong with me? All I could think of was her, and my eyes kept searching to see where she was and who she was spending time with. We kept our distance the following days. We hardly spoke.

On the day before last of the trip, we made it to the infamous Majdanek death camp, on the outskirts of the city of Lublin. The morning was nippy and damp, and the group members were visibly worn out.

While not the most famous of extermination camps, Majdanek felt strikingly different to me, when compared to the other camps we had visited. It reeked of evil. Located in the middle of a sprawling green field and surrounded by thick, evergreen forests, it is situated in close proximity to homes and community establishments. Ordinary people lived just outside the restored fences. Their parents and grandparents lived in those houses in the 1940s. Confronted by the towering crematorium chimney, there was no way to hide the atrocities that took place just hundreds of yards away from their breakfast tables. There was no way to deny the stench of human flesh burning, day and night, for years. The neighbors surely knew.

I took my time touring the campsite on my own for a few hours. The disturbing, diabolical scent I was sensing lingered as I crossed into the crematorium area and passed by the wooden guard tower overlooking the barbed-wire fence. Was it that aroma that unhinged me?

It was very cold, although I was wearing my thick winter coat. I started thinking of the forced laborers who were spared the gas chamber, and how a few managed to survive through months and years of this incredibly freezing cold, wearing a thin prisoner's uniform, malnourished, and considerably underweight. Growing up in a hot and humid climate, I had never connected the dots between freezing European winters and human survival in miserable concentration camp existence. The thought occurred to me that those kinds of realizations couldn't really emerge from reading encyclopedias about the war or hearing my grandfather's stories. I'd never felt that cold in my life before, and that thought stuck in my head. My body was literally shaking.

I remember getting angry, because I usually never got angry.

And then feeling confused about getting angry.

Why was I so upset? None of this information was new to me. I knew all about the six million of my people that had perished, by shooting, gassing, and other horrible ways. They all died a long time ago. This happened 30 years before I was born. I was losing my bearing.

Several people from our group were walking just ahead of me. Hannah was walking among them, alongside two other girls.

They went into the gas chamber building, and I joined them. I'd been exploring the science behind the massacre for years. The Germans used both carbon monoxide and Zyklon B, a cyanide-based pesticide, to murder inmates in the gas chambers, installed as public showers. The poor people were told they were going to wash themselves, and by the time they understood that lethal gas was being infused to the shower hall, they couldn't break out through the heavy metal doors. Zyklon B was eventually picked over the carbon monoxide because of its low cost and lethal efficiency. It worked faster on human bodies, especially in warmer temperatures. That's why the SS infused the gas after the victims took their hot showers. That morning, my eyes fixated on the blue-tinged marks left by the poisonous gas on the walls. My angst shot up, while the outside air temperature was further sinking.

The group exited, and I was left in the gas chamber. They walked through a gravel path to a row of ominous-looking wooden buildings that were recreated to look like the original barracks, used to store the clothing and valuables taken from Jews. The buildings were marked by the original signs written in German, indicating their functions.

Hannah and her two friends entered one of the buildings. I walked into that building a few minutes after them, still shaken up by the blue imprint on the walls and horrified by my revelation about the freezing cold temperatures.

The room was dark, the wooden floor creaking and screeching under my feet, the smell of evil blending with the malodor of tens of thousands of old shoes taken from victims, preserved in large containers at the back of the expansive space. Shrieking subtly from a dark corner was a silent weep. Turning my head towards the sound, I saw Hannah kneeling and crying.

"What happened? Are you okay?" I asked as I rushed to her and put my arm around her shoulder.

She pointed her hand to the corner of the room, which was barely lit.

"The hair, look at all their hair," she sobbed.

In the corner, hanging on the wall, was an old glass case filled with compressed human victim hair. Blond, white, black, and light brown.

"They gassed them all to death and then cut off their hair and kept it. What were they going to do with it?"

Was it that ghastly and terrible sight of decades-old human hair that followed hours of dark thoughts? Was it the warm feel of Hannah's tears? The amplified presence of evil, encircling and threatening to penetrate our souls? The snapshot of the blue walls? The freezing temperatures? Overwhelmed, I cracked.

I started feeling the freezing chills morphing into a pain deep in my gut, climbing very quickly up my esophagus and choking me. My breath shortened. Tears started coming down my eyes, and I couldn't speak. This had never happened to me before. I never cried.

I am not sure how long we were there, inseparable. It must have been several long minutes. At some point, I felt a tap on my shoulder. It was Ms. Zimmerman, drying a wet eye, asking us to join the team that was about to leave towards the bus.

A week later I was sitting with my grandfather in Netanya and telling him this story.

"My dear, I am happy you went on this trip," he said. "As you know, I put the past behind me in April of 1945. I decided that life was good, that positive thinking was the way to go and that if I don't take care of myself, no one else would. Now repeat after me – life is good."

"Life is good," I repeated.

"Positive thinking always," he continued.

"Positive thinking always," I repeated, like I had ever since I can remember myself on Grandpa Alex and Grandma Judith's wide bed after a Saturday family lunch.

"And if I don't take care of myself, no one else will."

"If I don't take care of myself, no one else will."

"While you were away, I did some thinking on my own. Would you like us to go to Weimar and visit my concentration camp? Not sure what's left of it. Now that the Berlin Wall has fallen, we are allowed to access the site. I've been suppressing any memory of those barracks for so many years but speaking with you about your Poland trip provided the spark I needed; it awakened a deep, idle memory."

"Are you sure you want to go back there, Grandfather? I read that not a lot is left from the original buildings."

"I am. Let's do this."

13 THE SMALL SQUARE II

Our flight landed early in the morning in Frankfurt, Germany. Grandfather was wearing his signature three-piece Hugo Boss suit and a wide, striped tie. He was ageless in his suits, tall and impressive. I wore a pair of wide Levi's jeans and a plain hoodie. If the world operated according to his life philosophy, we would all be walking the earth in three-piece suits and striped ties. I learned to accept his disappointment from my, and my generation's, pedestrian wardrobe choices, because he was generally content with my other choices.

We planned an aggressive itinerary for our Holocaust road trip, because of my school schedule. After spending the first day and night in Frankfurt, we planned to drive up to Weimar, spend a few hours around Buchenwald, then continue and cross the border to Prague in the afternoon. That's about seven hours on the road for one day. After 24 hours in the capital of Czechoslovakia, we were looking to drive to Brno to meet with a friend of Grandfather's from school, spend the night there, and in the morning make the long drive to Košice. We booked two nights there and thought about driving to Sečovce for one of the days. On the way back, we would drive to

Bratislava for a day, then cross the border to Vienna and fly back home.

Grandfather, always a modest man, usually rented low-profile cars on his trips abroad. He would drive an Opel Vectra or a Volkswagen Passat in Germany, never fussing about appearances or vying for attention. When we arrived at the Avis airport rental office, I was surprised to see a flashy black Mercedes 230E waiting for us.

"Nice car," I said. "Going to your old concentration camp in style, aren't we?"

He smiled and said nothing.

As a first order of business, Grandfather set up a meeting with his private banker at Frankfurter Sparkasse 1822 on the Zeil, in downtown, across the street from his favorite seafood fast-food joint, *NordSee*. A fundamental lesson for any survivor, he always said, was to never keep all their eggs, in terms of assets, in one basket, because any basket may become inaccessible at any given time, without prior notice.

"Can you imagine the value of our family's assets in Slovakia before the war? The land, farms, castles, real estate, stores... It's all gone, taken. European aristocracy, or descendants of Americans that came aboard the Mayflower are the world's rich people. In today's terms, our family would be billionaires. But under the clouds of war, all their assets were confiscated and never returned," he repeated the story I'd heard many times.

Being the sophisticated survivor, Grandfather spread around his assets, which he had earned in blood, sweat, and tears. I suspected that owning a German bank account was a mere excuse to pick up the phone and speak German to a service provider, every other week.

"Herr Funk, I'd like to introduce you to my grandson, Oren Schneider," he said, while proudly pushing me in front of the young banker. "Unfortunately, he doesn't speak German, but I know that your English is solid."

I knew he was in physical pain over the fact I wasn't wearing a suit, as I was stepping into the bank branch with him. He would be fine if it were not a three-piece suit, as long as it involved a tailored jacket. He couldn't help it. I explained to him that the fact I was not wearing suits did not mean I didn't love him more than anyone else in the world or respected him. It only meant that the year we lived in was 1992, not 1952 or 1932.

"Nice to meet you, Herr Schneider," Mr. Funk addressed me. "I'm sure this is not news to you, but your grandfather is a rather special individual, and we at the bank are lucky to have him as our loyal client for so many years."

"Believe me, Herr Funk, I know," I said, joining the kumbaya moment. "We all wish for him to remain a client and be able to visit you for many years to come."

"It would be an honor for the bank," he said, smiling. "If I may ask, what brings you both to Germany this week? Business or pleasure, or both?"

"Good question. I'm not sure the motive falls into either. We are returning to visit Mr. Ružiak's concentration camp, where he was imprisoned as a forced laborer until his liberation in 1945," I answered without mincing words.

Young Mr. Funk most possibly experienced a mild stroke. He switched colors, coughed lightly, and somehow composed himself after a few seconds.

"I see," he replied. He paused and coughed again. "I had no idea. I am so sorry to learn about this, Herr Ružiak. I feel terrible."

"Now, now, Herr Funk," said Grandfather, who didn't like this dynamic at all. "My grandson should not have mentioned this. Let's let bygones be bygones, everything is fine. This is ancient history, a different life, and a different person. I just wanted to show my grandson the place that to some extent made me the person I am today and that impacted the person that he has become."

"Dearest Herr Ružiak, I am terribly sorry for the past. As you know, our generation has to accept the terrible history of our people and do our best to correct and pay for our forefathers' mistakes. I wish you many years of health and prosperity with your family." He shook our hands, and we went out.

"I make it a point never to speak of the dark past with them," Grandfather said as we were wolfing down a herring sandwich outside. "Did you really have to mention this to Funk?"

"Yes. Well, no, but he asked me. And there is really no reason to hide it. There are generations of people in this country who have been forced to confront the evils of their ancestors. It's part of who they are. Herr Funk seems like a nice, educated, and intelligent person. He deserves to be told."

The second order of business in Frankfurt was the visit to Uncle Bella, my Great-grandmother Irena's young brother. He lived alone in Frankfurt under his WWII nom de guerre, Michal Kazimir. Grandfather and I walked to Bella's apartment from the Zeil, rang his doorbell, and were buzzed in. Bella was thin, much shorter than his beloved nephew, and reminded me of Albert Einstein with his thick eyebrows and thinning, white combed-back hair. He was very excited to see his favorite nephew, with whom he shared a deep bond, unique to survivors of war and atrocities. They spoke in Hungarian, and Grandfather translated.

"Sanyi, I'm so happy to see both of you. I rarely see any people nowadays, with both my daughters and ex-wife living far away from me. I wanted to ask your grandson if he had interest in taking my stamp collection. I have no one to take over this project."

We flipped through one of his albums, and I gracefully declined.

"Can you imagine Gorbachev and the idiots in Moscow?" Bella said. "The crooked and corrupt politburo screwed up an entire movement. They have become capitalists, privatizing the greatest proletariat industrial complex ever established. I'm so sad about it, Sanyi, the world is collapsing around us, suffocated by oligarchs and private enterprise."

"You look good, Bella. I'm happy to hear you are sticking to your guns and ideology, and keeping us capitalists honest." Both men laughed like old friends, united after years of separation.

"It's good that you are taking your grandson to visit the camp. All young people should see what the fascists did and know that history is bound to repeat itself. Young man," Bella turned and faced me, his smile all but gone and said, "don't be impressed by the riches of the world, as beneath them lie the most foul and prosaic of barbarian human instincts and desires. What happened to our generation can easily happen to yours unless you keep your guard up. Don't be afraid to stand up to evil!"

"Now, now, Uncle. The world is very different now and none of us is at risk of annihilation," Grandfather attempted to lighten up the atmosphere.

We stayed there for another hour, and I listened to the old men telling tales of the past. The two survivors from a different era looked comfortable in the company of each other. I hoped it wouldn't be the last time we visited Bella, our very own war hero.

The third order of business in Frankfurt was the nocturnal *Eisbein* ceremony. Grandfather was never known to be fussy about food, and was, in fact, no culinary standout by any standard. However, when sitting in front of an *Eisbein* [boiled and cured German pork knuckle], you could see the young, passionate Alexander come out, excitement and lust in his eyes. Since childhood, he would drag us around Germany and Austria in search of the ultimate preparation for this delicacy, also known as the *Schweinshaxe*. It was usually roasted, crispy skinned, served with mashed potatoes or pea purée and sauerkraut, with a squirt of quality mustard. His quest led him to identify the Frankfurt neighborhood of Sachsenhausen as the mecca of *Eisbein*. We spent the evening at Zum Gemalten Haus, and Grandfather got his fix.

"Are you nervous about tomorrow?" I asked.

"A little bit," he answered, dismembering any last pieces of meat off the knuckle. "I hope something is left there to see. It's as if I need to be reassured it was all real."

"Well, all your stories are going to live for generations when I write them down. Dinner just reminded me of your and Opapa's pork meal in camp shortly after liberation. No one can take these stories away."

We toasted one last time with some local *Weissbier*, and headed back to the hotel, to rest before the early start the next morning.

The trip to Weimar took a little longer than three hours. Our luxury means of transportation was very pleasant, and Grandfather was driving as fast as 190 kilometers per hour. The wide and smooth, no-speed-limit autobahn disappeared when we crossed to the former East Germany, where the highways were an aggregation of huge concrete plates. He slowed the car down considerably.

We passed the city of Weimar, followed the signs to the historic site, and turned into the parking lot of the Buchenwald Memorial. Grandfather parked, and I could see he was anxious. It was a cold day, but we were well dressed and prepared.

Under the clock tower, in the main entrance, JEDEM DAS SEINE still read the words on the gate.

We entered a wide, mostly empty area. None of the wooden sleep barracks was standing, and there were small, black rocks neatly lined, marking the dimensions of those buildings, frozen in time, as if it was April 1945. The crematorium building and chimney stood like an orphan in the middle of nothing. Grandfather walked ahead, and I followed him.

"This is where the Small Square, the alternate parade ground, stood, in front of the administration building," he said. "This is where the SS officer almost killed me before my father and Günter saved my life."

"How do you feel about standing here, today?"

"Honestly, I have spent my entire life suppressing the feelings I felt as a teenager, while experiencing the events I've been telling you about. I think of young Alexander Rosenberg and his father Solomon Rosenberg, malnourished and pathetic in their stinky prisoner clothes, fighting for their survival here, as book or movie characters, not as suffering humans."

"Do you ever regret any of the family's decisions or actions back then, during the war, after you knew that the Germans were looking to annihilate all Jews?"

"No, I've no regrets because that's not what our family is about. We always look forward, never backwards. My one and only thought that resembles regret, but is not really that, is about not taking a boat trip to Ellis Island instead of the one we took to Jaffa. But I followed my love, and now we have all of you in our lives, and I don't regret that for one second. The war period taught me many lessons, which I've been sharing with you since birth. If we didn't truly believe we'd make it out alive, we wouldn't have. Positive thinking is the foundation of life, and a core muscle that needs constant flexing and everyday exercise. Self-dependence is another notable muscle. If I don't take care of myself, no one else will. Life is good for me because my bar was reset to its lowest level in 1941, and then in 1942, and then in 1943, and then in 1944, and then in 1945. Compared to those years of adolescence, life has been heavenly. So, as you can see, I have no regrets."

Grandfather was silent during the drive to Prague, the border crossing, and passport control. The proud capital city, very soon to become the capital of the divided Czech Republic, looked tired and beaten, its historic monuments neglected and worn-out. We arrived late to the Forum Hotel and immediately went to sleep. When I woke up in the morning, he was already showered and dressed, operating his electric shaver, his exaggerated "Davidoff Cool Water" cologne causing me to block my nose.

"You look like you slept well. Put on your clothes, let's grab a quick breakfast and get on the road. Can't wait to visit Zdenek after almost 50 years." He was becoming restless.

An hour later we were on the road to Brno, located two hours southeast of the capital. Zdenek Šuba studied together with Grandfather after the war in Bratislava during the one year he went to school there, and they kept in touch through the years through letters and a once-in-a-decade phone call. Zdenek became an engineer and worked for a defense factory under the communist regime, which also limited his ability to leave the country. Grandfather had Zdenek's address written on an old piece of paper, and he stopped an ancient, toothless woman on the side streets of Brno to ask for directions. She pointed towards a distant project block with dozens of Soviet-style gray concrete high-rises.

The black Mercedes Benz seemed out of place when parallel parked in a row of old white Russian Ladas. We went into a dark foyer reeking of state-produced disinfectants and stepped into a very small, noisy elevator that took us up to the ninth floor with notable effort and mechanical screeches.

Zdenek had white hair, a face stained with sunspots, and multiple missing teeth. He looked 20 years older than Grandfather, although they were about the same age. The two men, who hadn't seen each other since 1947, hugged lengthily and spoke in passionate Slovak. Every few minutes, I received a summarized translation.

"The apartments in these buildings are leased by the government to retired, senior state employees. At the age of 58, Zdenek retired and moved here, shortly after the unfortunate and untimely death of his poor wife, who died of cancer."

"He is living on a government stipend of 30 dollars per month. This suffices to cover food, clothes, and transportation, but not a lot more."

"Here, look at these photographs taken while Zdenek was managing electrical projects in Cuba during the 60s."

"He says the economy is collapsing, unemployment is very high, and the state services, like healthcare and education, have been gradually deteriorating."

I enjoyed an iced tea and local biscuits as the men spent a fair amount of time catching up. Zdenek's apartment was small, his wooden and straw furniture old but well kept. On the living room cabinet there were a number of detailed model freight ships built inside bottles. Apparently Zdenek had a nautical hobby. Next to them was a 16-inch tubular, black-and-white television, and a radio transistor was playing classical music at low volume on AM radio waves in the kitchen.

At some point Grandfather stood up, took out his wallet, counted ten bills of 100 dollars and handed them over to Zdenek, who couldn't hide his excitement.

"He needs to undergo multiple tooth transplants, which is only done in a private dental clinic in Brno, and he couldn't afford it, so I volunteered to help," he explained to me.

They hugged again and we left. It was getting dark, and we drove to a rather shabby hotel in the center of the city.

"How the Soviets ruined this country, and every other country they took over after the war," said Grandfather while offering our passports to the receptionist. "Brno used to be a center of manufacturing and trade, with beautiful intellectuals debating philosophy in cafes. It's a rundown shithole now. That's what I always tell Uncle Bella, communism is a beautiful idea that can't work, because people are involved."

Nothing actually worked in our archaic, dusty honeymoon suite, the best rental space the hotel had to offer. Water didn't come out of the faucet. The light wouldn't turn on. The chair collapsed as soon as I sat on it. The rusty window hinge broke when I tried to roll it open. There was no maintenance service in the hotel after four o'clock in the afternoon.

We sat in the room and opened a bottle of lukewarm local sparkling water, because the mini-fridge was out of order.

"Zdenek was the smartest, wittiest person in our school; everyone loved him," he reminisced. "Had he managed to leave this place before the communists took over and go to America, he could have been a multimillionaire system developer and cofounder of a company like Xerox, HP, Bell Labs, or IBM. Still, he is one of the lucky state pensioners here. Most of our classmates at the time became penniless factory workers."

The next day we continued our road trip across the frosty fields of Slovakia, en route to the capital of the East, Košice. For

Grandfather, this was his childhood metropolis, with its wide pedestrian areas, cinemas, fancy coffee shops, bakeries, and multiple businesses owned by close and distant family members. This was where he had fallen in love and found his life partner. Now this city had turned into a gloomy, blue-collar town, with its dilapidated concrete neighborhoods and crumbling utilities. Our hotel seemed similar in standard to the one we just escaped from early in the morning in Brno. He asked the concierge to recommend an authentic Eastern Slovak kitchen nearby. For years, he had been itching to watch me devour his childhood delicacies. Hearing numerous stories about the legendary local sheep milk cheese, the *bryndza*, I could almost taste the *bryndzové halušky* [cheese dumplings], his most vivid memory from home cooking. To his disappointment, when we sat down at the small restaurant, which took us almost an hour to locate and arrive at, we were told that they were all out of cheese. We ended up munching on hearty and satisfying bowls of fatty goulash soups.

In the morning we drove to Sečovce.

Since forever, I recalled hearing stories about the Rosenbergs' hometown: the large house, the Solomon Rosenberg specialty store, the beautiful furniture, the rich social life, the Jewish community, the family, the friends, the rise of the *Garda*, the waves of antisemitism, the horrible day of Jewish deportation, and the escape to Michalovce. I imagined a magical small town, with old Italian-style townhouses, engulfed and conquered by evil 50 years back.

As we were driving and getting close, I spotted the first Gypsy caravans and horses at the side of the road. Until then, I had only read about Gypsies in books and seen movies that depicted their traditional clothing with musical instruments and domesticated animals. There they were in front of us, completely real and authentic. I asked Grandfather to stop the car so I could get a better look. Almost immediately after we pulled over, two angry-looking men, one whose face was scarred from ear to ear, started approaching us in rapid steps. He didn't wait for them to come any closer, and promptly drove away.

"Did Gypsies always live here?" I asked.

"Yes. I remember them here, around the same fields, since I was born. They were chased, persecuted, captured, deported, and annihilated, like the Jews, in the 30s and 40s. I guess that the ones who survived came back to their homeland after the war."

We drove into town. The magical small town living in my visions was replaced with a poor, ramshackle rural community, almost deprived of any inhabitants. He steered the car towards 152 Štefánikova Street and stopped right in front of the address. The old family house that hosted the family business was no longer there. The lot now hosted an ugly concrete structure and featured a lot of debris and garbage, like many other lots around.

"Nothing left, they demolished the house," he said nonchalantly.

We got out of the car, and he stepped onto the lot. "Here is where the house stood." He walked swiftly along the curb, his hands marking the building's boundaries. "This is where the store entrance was located. But it's gone. All of the pretty houses are gone. This sleepy and ugly place is nothing like the street I grew up in."

"But this property belongs to you! Did you ever ask to get it back after the war?" I asked.

"I don't care for this lot. I want nothing to do with it. Let the locals choke on it."

There was not a lot left to say. He was emotionless, almost expecting to find nothing where the house he was born in once stood. "There's only one person I need to visit before we leave. Let's head down to the Jewish cemetery, if it's still there."

We drove to the outskirts of town until we arrived at a tree-lined street with a tall, rusted fence running in parallel to the road. At the center of the fence was a large, rusted metal Star of David. Inside, the ground was covered with wild, high chrysanthemum bushes. Between them were crooked white gravestones of different heights, colors, and shapes. Some were completely ripped and crushed, others were in better condition, with readable inscriptions. The gate was locked, and Grandfather knocked on the door of the adjacent house.

He explained that there was typically a family of gatekeepers living in the house nearest to the cemetery. He was right. An old woman came out, and after a short dialogue and a cash contribution from the visitor, she accompanied us to the gate and unlocked it. We went in and started walking between the graves. For almost 50 years, no funerals or yahrzeit ceremonies had taken place here. Families of the people buried here were, for the most part, murdered during the Holocaust. Unlike their ancestors, those family members were not buried in marked graves.

A few moments later, I was standing in front of the grave of my great-great grandfather, Bernat Rosenberg, whose Hebrew name was Dov. The gravestone said in Hebrew:

Here rests
Our glorious Rabbi and teacher
Dov Rosenberg
Son of the renowned,
genius Rabbi of Tăşnad,
Solomon Katz Rosenberg
Chose he the righteous path
Acquired a crown of glory and good name
A dear son to his parents
His soul dedicated and heart pure
Charity and kindness led his way.

"He died just months before I was born, I never got to meet him, but I was always told stories about his life. He was a true entrepreneur, who renounced the religious Orthodox lifestyle, created the family's wealth, and shared it with the Jewish community of Sečovce," said Grandfather. "At least we could say we didn't travel all the way here for naught."

We took a few photos using his new, digital Pentax camera, and got back in the car.

The next morning, we started our long drive west, towards the soon-to-become capital of the independent state of Slovakia, and towards Bratislava, the place where he and his parents were turned over by a Jewish snitch to the Nazis.

It was raining heavily throughout our time there, so we mainly toured the notable family memorial sites by car. We drove past the apartment building where my great-grandmother Theresia Rosenbaum had hidden with her daughter Gisella. We located the street and house where the family had rented a unit from Marika and had been picked up by the Gestapo twice, having been given away by the informer. We identified the commercial building where the Miroslav Schweska typewriter agency once operated. The agency was no longer there. We stopped outside the large, empty-looking building on Kozia Street that served as the SS transfer facility, where the family was brought to before being marched to the train station and deported to Germany. He was relatively unemotional and reserved that whole day, as if he was showing off someone else's trail of capture.

"Okay! I've seen enough of my homeland," said Grandfather. "It's a shame how backwards everything turned out here after the war. I'm very happy we came and feel privileged to have had the opportunity to take you through the story, step by step, chapter by chapter. But now, let's please go back to civilization... I can't wait to get to Vienna tomorrow, sleep in a proper hotel, enjoy fresh, nice smelling sheets, and do some suit and tie shopping."

He did score a win later that night when the hotel restaurant served us my first ever portion of *bryndzové halušky*.

"Wow, this is so salty and fatty." The first bite kicked me. "No wonder this memory was so vivid and carved in your mind."

"Right? Isn't it great?" He smiled and missed the nuance.

"Yes, you can definitely get used to it. You honestly never had your favorite childhood dish since before you left with Grandmother to Israel, at the age of 21?"

"I did have it in Austria a couple of times, but nothing like the original recipe. I guess that my erase-and-rewind mechanism also diminished my craving for it. I can definitely get used to these dumplings again!"

We crossed over the border to Austria in the morning and spent the day between department stores and museums in beautiful Vienna.

That evening he took me to one of his all-time favorite restaurants, an old-school Hungarian joint he had been frequenting on his business trips for decades. Obviously, jackets and ties were obligatory.

We sat down, and I started reading the menu using my very basic German.

He was looking in all directions and seemed distracted.

"What's wrong?" I asked.

"Oh, nothing. They usually have the Gypsy band here on Wednesdays. Ah, yes, I can see them on the other side of the hall. It's all good now."

"Waiter!" He gestured to a well-dressed, old gentleman, who approached us as gracefully as a ballet dancer. "Please make sure the musicians come here next," he said and gave him two 100-schilling bills.

Within two minutes, five Gypsy musicians circled our table, focusing their eyes at the patron. Their leader was holding a violin. The others had two additional violins, a double bass, and a bulky cimbalom.

Grandfather and the head violinist spoke in Hungarian and then moved to Slovak. They seemed like brothers, separated at birth, neighbors from a different space and time, reunited to speak a universal tongue of string tunes. I assumed they were reviewing the potential playlist for the evening and building the dinner repertoire.

The lead musician gave the sign, and the band kicked in. They played dozens of melodies, some sounded familiar, others didn't. The guest of honor was on cloud nine, singing his lungs out. I ordered us food and beer and took pleasure in seeing the violins connecting him to those deep places in his childhood, where not even Sečovce or Buchenwald were able to take him to.

And then a strain of tunes came out, and even I recognized *Under our window* as played by young Alexander to his mother and her friends, a lifetime ago, in a different universe, one with elegant cigarette holders and mink furs, before the Nazis came to town. And he sang:

> *Under our window,*
> *tends to be very cold.*
> *Our well is frozen,*
> *and water isn't flowing.*

> *I'll take my little hatchet,*
> *and break the ice layer.*
> *And in our well,*
> *water will flow again.*

> *Under our window,*
> *Is a white rose flower.*
> *Tell me, my dear,*
> *What troubles you so.*

> *I'll take my little hatchet,*
> *and break the ice layer.*
> *And in our well,*
> *water will flow again.*

> *Under our window,*
> *a white Lilia.*
> *Tell me, my dear,*
> *who comes for you.*

> *I'll take my little hatchet,*

and break the ice layer.
And in our well,
water will flow again.

The Gypsy band leader couldn't hide his own excitement. Not every day did he encounter a fellow music aficionado from the old motherland, this one also came with a stash of Austrian schillings that just kept piling up on the table.

The waiter was pleased. Guests around were glued to the scene of a well-dressed, white- haired, handsome old man singing with his nightingale voice and holding on to the band with a mountain of bills. Food and beer kept on coming out from the kitchen. Thank God for Alexander Ružiak, every night he showed up was a good night for business.

The tears slid down his face, and for one sticky, smelly hour in a steaming Hungarian cellar, serving greasy, rural Slovak cuisine in faraway Vienna, he was again Alexander, the only child, the musician from Sečovce, who collected exotic stamps, loved his dad's store, excelled at being a technical apprentice, and dreamt of distant lands that produced exciting herbs and spices.

14 EPILOGUE

FEBRUARY 2020, BROOKLYN, NEW YORK, USA

"Hi Oren, it's Grandpa Alex," he said, starting the call the same way every time, as if I didn't know who it was after hearing his first breath. The weight of the years could be heard in his slower pronunciation and lower voice, but his mind was as sharp as ever.

"Hi Grandpa," I answered, taking my eyes off the computer screen and the spreadsheet and put down the iPhone.

"Am I calling you at a bad time? Are you busy at work?" he asked, continuing the same way. In his mind, work always came first.

"No, it's fine. How are you feeling? How is rehab going?"

While visiting him in Netanya just a few weeks earlier in December, he had fallen, fractured his femur bone, and undergone reconstructive surgery. He wasn't yet able to walk and had started a rehabilitation process.

"It's hard because I'm so weak. I wanted to hear your voice one last time and bid you farewell. I don't know how much more time I have left."

"Grandpa, you've been saying this to me for more than 15 years, and still here we are. Your brain is sharp, and your body will regain its strength with practice and work. You must get better so we can all see you when we visit in March. The girls miss your magic show."

"I hope so. If we don't see each other again, know that I love you and that I am proud and happy about your life choices and decisions. Take good care of the French dogs. They traveled a long way from where they were created."

"Don't worry, Grandpa. Work hard on your rehab so we can see each other in March."

He will be fine. He has always been fine. Life taught him to be resilient and independent, and how to survive. Even after the horrendous Asia financial crisis of 1998, when he had thought all his life's work was going down the drain, and dreams about Nazi captors haunted his sleep every night, he managed to land on his robust two feet.

That same day he called, the *New York Times* continued reporting that the mysterious virus that attacked the community of Wuhan, China, was now rampant in Italy and Spain. A few weeks later, the COVID-19 outbreak in New York City forced me to shut down my business and furlough all our US and global staff. Frantic negotiations with investors, lenders, landlords, and others pursued. We were quarantining at home, and I was fighting for our economic survival.

"We were not allowed to see Grandfather Alex today. Due to COVID, the facility is not open to families," my sister texted me.

I tried calling his number. There was no answer.

"Can we ask a staff member to help him get on a call with one of us? I want to hear his voice and make sure he's doing okay," I texted back.

"It's COVID madness here, the staff is unresponsive. They are dealing with an outbreak in the facility, and no one is returning my call," she answered.

For an entire week, we were unable to speak with him.

My anxiety over Grandfather's situation mixed with the tension of a cash-strapped business, laying off employees, helping the girls troubleshoot online access problems while remote learning from home, and sanitizing grocery shipments. I thought to myself that there couldn't be a worse time to be old and sick, and tried not to think too much about him, lying in his bed at the medical facility, alone.

It was late March when my sister gave me a call.

"I just heard from the doctor. Grandfather passed away peacefully yesterday in the sealed department. He didn't suffer from COVID, he was just alone, in solitude, away from all of us, and decided he'd had enough. He will not even get to have a proper burial ceremony, and I know you won't be able to get here, being locked down in Brooklyn."

I walked over to the living room, picked up the bronze statue of two wide-eyed, long-eared French bulldogs, standing and gazing towards the horizon, and sat on the couch.

"Are you sad, Daddy?" asked Rio, my oldest daughter, who climbed up with a technical problem with her laptop.

I was at a loss for words.

"Don't worry, I know things are hard, but life is good, you must think positively and remember: If you don't take care of yourself, no one else will take care of you," she told me as she hugged me, as if he had spoken to me through her soft voice.

Descendants of Bernat Yehoshua Dov Rosenberg and Hannah Grun
(Sečovce)

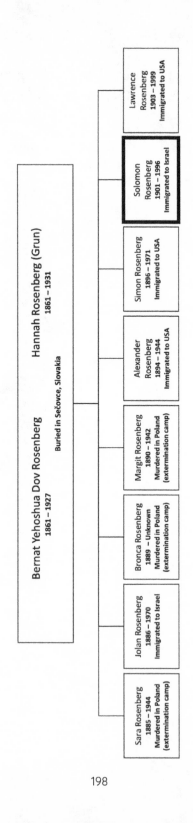

Descendants of Alexander Rosenbaum and Theresia Markovic (Michalovce)

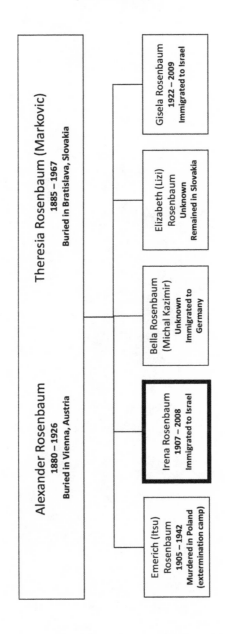

PHOTOS

Solomon Rosenberg (late 1920s)

Alexander Rosenberg (1929)

Alexander Rosenberg and Grandma Rosenbaum
(1934)

The Buchenwald certificate with Alex's photo (1945)

Alexander in workshop (1947)

From Left to Right: Alexander, Judith, Solomon, Irena
(1948)

Alexander and Judith (1948)

Alex Ruziak and Oren Schneider (1977)

Bernat Dov Rosenberg's (great-great grandfather)
tombstone in Sečovce (1992)

The Jewish cemetery in Sečovce (1992)

Alexander (2004)

Alexander and Oren (2019)

ABOUT THE AUTHOR

Oren Schneider was born in Israel, a third generation to Holocaust survivors and seventh generation to farmers from the Galilee. He is an entrepreneur who enjoys music, cooking, travel, people and especially the combination of all four. He lives with his family in Brooklyn.

AMSTERDAM PUBLISHERS HOLOCAUST LIBRARY

The series **Holocaust Survivor Memoirs World War II** consists of the following autobiographies of survivors:

Outcry. Holocaust Memoirs, by Manny Steinberg

Hank Brodt Holocaust Memoirs. A Candle and a Promise, by Deborah Donnelly

The Dead Years. Holocaust Memoirs, by Joseph Schupack

Rescued from the Ashes. The Diary of Leokadia Schmidt, Survivor of the Warsaw Ghetto, by Leokadia Schmidt

My Lvov. Holocaust Memoir of a twelve-year-old Girl, by Janina Hescheles

Remembering Ravensbrück. From Holocaust to Healing, by Natalie Hess

Wolf. A Story of Hate, by Zeev Scheinwald with Ella Scheinwald

Save my Children. An Astonishing Tale of Survival and its Unlikely Hero, by Leon Kleiner with Edwin Stepp

Holocaust Memoirs of a Bergen-Belsen Survivor & Classmate of Anne Frank, by Nanette Blitz Konig

Defiant German - Defiant Jew. A Holocaust Memoir from inside the Third Reich, by Walter Leopold with Les Leopold

In a Land of Forest and Darkness. The Holocaust Story of two Jewish Partisans, by Sara Lustigman Omelinski

Holocaust Memories. Annihilation and Survival in Slovakia, by Paul Davidovits

From Auschwitz with Love. The Inspiring Memoir of Two Sisters' Survival, Devotion and Triumph Told by Manci Grunberger Beran & Ruth Grunberger Mermelstein, by Daniel Seymour

Remetz. Resistance Fighter and Survivor of the Warsaw Ghetto, by Jan Yohay Remetz

My March Through Hell. A Young Girl's Terrifying Journey to Survival, by Halina Kleiner with Edwin Stepp

———

The series **Holocaust Survivor True Stories WWII** consists of the following biographies:

Among the Reeds. The true story of how a family survived the Holocaust, by Tammy Bottner

A Holocaust Memoir of Love & Resilience. Mama's Survival from Lithuania to America, by Ettie Zilber

Living among the Dead. My Grandmother's Holocaust Survival Story of Love and Strength, by Adena Bernstein Astrowsky

Heart Songs. A Holocaust Memoir, by Barbara Gilford

Shoes of the Shoah. The Tomorrow of Yesterday, by Dorothy Pierce

Hidden in Berlin. A Holocaust Memoir, by Evelyn Joseph Grossman

Separated Together. The Incredible True WWII Story of Soulmates Stranded an Ocean Apart, by Kenneth P. Price, Ph.D.

The Man Across the River. The incredible story of one man's will to survive the Holocaust, by Zvi Wiesenfeld

If Anyone Calls, Tell Them I Died. A Memoir, by Emanuel (Manu) Rosen

The House on Thrömerstrasse. A Story of Rebirth and Renewal in the Wake of the Holocaust, by Ron Vincent

Dancing with my Father. His hidden past. Her quest for truth. How Nazi Vienna shaped a family's identity, by Jo Sorochinsky

The Story Keeper. Weaving the Threads of Time and Memory - A Memoir, by Fred Feldman

Krisia's Silence. The Girl who was not on Schindler's List, by Ronny Hein

Defying Death on the Danube. A Holocaust Survival Story, by Debbie J. Callahan with Henry Stern

A Doorway to Heroism. A decorated German-Jewish Soldier who became an American Hero, by Rabbi W. Jack Romberg

The Shoemaker's Son. The Life of a Holocaust Resister, by Laura Beth Bakst

The Redhead of Auschwitz. A True Story, by Nechama Birnbaum

Land of Many Bridges. My Father's Story, by Bela Ruth Samuel Tenenholtz

Creating Beauty from the Abyss. The Amazing Story of Sam Herciger, Auschwitz Survivor and Artist, by Lesley Ann Richardson

On Sunny Days We Sang. A Holocaust Story of Survival and Resilience, by Jeannette Grunhaus de Gelman

Painful Joy. A Holocaust Family Memoir, by Max J. Friedman

I Give You My Heart. A True Story of Courage and Survival, by Wendy Holden

In the Time of Madmen, by Mark A. Prelas

Monsters and Miracles. Horror, Heroes and the Holocaust, by Ira Wesley Kitmacher

Flower of Vlora. Growing up Jewish in Communist Albania, by Anna Kohen

Aftermath: Coming of Age on Three Continents. A Memoir, by Annette Libeskind Berkovits

Not a real Enemy. The True Story of a Hungarian Jewish Man's Fight for Freedom, by Robert Wolf

Zaidy's War. Four Armies, Three Continents, Two Brothers. One Man's Impossible Story of Endurance, by Martin Bodek

The Glassmaker's Son. Looking for the World my Father left behind in Nazi Germany, by Peter Kupfer

The Apprentice of Buchenwald. The True Story of the Teenage Boy Who Sabotaged Hitler's War Machine, by Oren Schneider

The Cello Still Sings. A Generational Story of the Holocaust and of the Transformative Power of Music, by Janet Horvath

---

The series **Jewish Children in the Holocaust** consists of the following autobiographies of Jewish children hidden during WWII in the Netherlands:

Searching for Home. The Impact of WWII on a Hidden Child, by Joseph Gosler

See You Tonight and Promise to be a Good Boy! War memories, by Salo Muller

Sounds from Silence. Reflections of a Child Holocaust Survivor, Psychiatrist and Teacher, by Robert Krell

Sabine's Odyssey. A Hidden Child and her Dutch Rescuers, by Agnes Schipper

The Journey of a Hidden Child, by Harry Pila and Robin Black

The series **New Jewish Fiction** consists of the following novels, written by Jewish authors. All novels are set in the time during or after the Holocaust.

The Corset Maker. A Novel, by Annette Libeskind Berkovits

Escaping the Whale. The Holocaust is over. But is it ever over for the next generation? by Ruth Rotkowitz

When the Music Stopped. Willy Rosen's Holocaust, by Casey Hayes

Hands of Gold. One Man's Quest to Find the Silver Lining in Misfortune, by Roni Robbins

The Girl Who Counted Numbers. A Novel, by Roslyn Bernstein

There was a garden in Nuremberg. A Novel, by Navina Michal Clemerson

The Butterfly and the Axe, by Omer Bartov

Good for a Single Journey, by Helen Joyce

The series **Holocaust Books for Young Adults** consists of the following novels, based on true stories:

The Boy behind the Door. How Salomon Kool Escaped the Nazis. Inspired by a True Story, by David Tabatsky

Running for Shelter. A True Story, by Suzette Sheft

The Precious Few. An Inspirational Saga of Courage based on True Stories, by David Twain with Art Twain

Jacob's Courage: A Holocaust Love Story, by Charles S. Weinblatt

---

The series **WW2 Historical Fiction** consists of the following novels, some of which are based on true stories:

Mendelevski's Box. A Heartwarming and Heartbreaking Jewish Survivor's Story, by Roger Swindells

A Quiet Genocide. The Untold Holocaust of Disabled Children WW2 Germany, by Glenn Bryant

The Knife-Edge Path, by Patrick T. Leahy

Brave Face. The Inspiring WWII Memoir of a Dutch/German Child, by I. Caroline Crocker and Meta A. Evenly

When We Had Wings. The Gripping Story of an Orphan in Janusz Korczak's Orphanage. A Historical Novel, by Tami Shem-Tov

Want to be an AP book reviewer?

Reviews are very important in a world dominated by the social media and social proof. Please drop us a line if you want to join the *AP review team*. We will then add you to our list of advance reviewers. No strings attached, and we promise that we will not be spamming you.

info@amsterdampublishers.com

CPSIA information can be obtained
at www.ICGtesting.com
Printed in the USA
LVHW011639220523
747675LV00003B/479